Where Would I Be?

Where Would I Be?

THE LIFE AND TIMES
OF IRENE CLARK WARD

Peggie Ward Koon, Ph.D.

To order additional copies of this book, contact:
Xlibris Corporation
1-888-795-4274
www.Xlibris.com
Orders@Xlibris.com
21081

Contents

TO MOTHER WITH LOVE

Forward

An article, "The Children on Cherry Avenue", by Sylvia Cooper, appeared in the Augusta Chronicle newspaper early last year. The article's focus was the children that grew up on Cherry Avenue, a street down in Hornsby Subdivision— one of Augusta's oldest black neighborhoods. All of these children were successful, pursued higher education, and are now productive citizens who are making positive contributions to society. About now, you're probably wondering, well why should it be of concern to me? You see I am one of the Cherry Avenue *kids* in the article. The article carefully reviewed each of the households on the street, including the one where I grew up, querying why and how all these children turned out so well. The question had never crossed my mind. A brief statement was included about the heads of each household, including my Mother, Irene Ward, who had ten children of her own. My Mother and my Father, Enoch Ward (now deceased), lived in the house on the corner of Cherry Avenue and Rachael Street.

Several of the households were described in the article; the gist of these descriptions can be summarized as follows. First and foremost, the family unit was cited as the single most important influence on the children in that neighborhood; all of the households on that street had the traditional father and mother as a married couple in tact. This black neighborhood's typical household was compared in contrast to today's typical black household, one that is characterized by SMS or the "Single Mom Syndrome". The author writes in what appears to be *amazement* that despite America's tendency to stereotype black families, in the 1950's and '60's each household in this little black area of Augusta, Georgia, was the epitome of the *American* family unit, with both parents actively involved in the proper upbringing of their children. More often than not, the mother was at home while the father was hard at work; and the children, though they were black and far from affluent, grew up in an environment entrenched in traditional American family values.

As the reporter interviewed my brother, Rev. Enoch Ward, Jr., and me about my Mother, we answered candidly questions about her strong but loving hand in our lives. On reflection, I often wonder *where I would be* if she had not been there to guide me; my siblings and I often sit and reminisce about the fun and the discipline that we experienced as children. Yes, it was a time filled with struggles and trials that included good times and bad; we dealt with harsh realities that involved racism and exclusion. But there were plenty of opportunities for achievement and advancement. She lovingly led us by example, onward and upward to better things. It was the good life!

Last year I turned 50 and my Mother, Irene Ward reached the age of 90. Neither Mother nor any of my siblings live in the old house at the corner of Cherry Avenue and Rachael Street. It's the Saturday before Mother's Day, May 10, 2003 and I just spent the day with my Mom at her new residence, a local Nursing Home. Today, I saw my 90-year-old Mother in a wheel chair sitting with that big encouraging smile, still determined to look and be her best at everything that she does. I returned to my home thinking how very blessed I am to have her as my Mother. Throughout my entire life, she has been there for me (and my siblings)—to encourage, to console, to chastise, to defend, to lecture, to share, to support, to admonish, and to love *me—Where would I be* . . . without her?

But this book is not just about my Mother's influence on me. It is about the life that she has lived and the legacy that she leaves to all those whose lives she has touched for 90 years. This book is the true story of Irene Clark Ward, the first-born daughter of James and Ina Mae Clark. It is an exposé that includes the contents of my mother's personal journal, which she kept until she reached 88 years old and could no longer hold pen in hand, along with details of personal conversations about her past that she shared with me. It speaks volumes about her background, her character and her spirit. "*Where would I Be?*" is the story of one amazing matriarch whose lifetime spanned so much of history—a woman who will forever be loved and cherished by all who have been touched by her for as long as we live!

Peggie Ward Koon, Ph.D.

The Birth Rite

When I think of the South I think of home. The old South that I remember as a child was full of beautiful countryside with wide-open spaces and red clay dirt roads. Wild flowers grew in bunches along the roadside; as you walked you could see rows of cotton, peanuts, corn, peas, beans, and other crops that were grown in abundance. Wild berries, which were un-poisoned by insecticides or other contaminants, were picked and eaten right off the vine. People ate the vegetables that they grew; the animals that they raised were fed naturally. I never heard my Mother tell me about "*safely handling*" chicken, pork, or beef when we prepared it for cooking; and there were no known reports of getting sick from ecoli bacteria. People lived in houses that were made of planks of wood with very little insulation. We enjoyed talking to each other face to face; and although we walked miles to see a friend or family member we did not tire. There were few doctors available, and when we got sick my Mother would make a home remedy to cure us; there were no aspirins or Anacin's to take every four hours for the pain. It was a beautiful place and time—a simple life with so few of the conveniences and complexities we have today. And yet the South was a place of bitterness, hatred, and death for many black folk—young and old.

After the Civil War Black folk who had been emancipated from slavery were still recovering from the psychological and economic effects of the process. According to many it was a time of confusion for our race; freedom was not always welcome. "How will we live without our Master?", some would ask. Many remained in farming as sharecroppers on Southern plantations. Some would flee north—only to be disappointed by a new kind of enslavement. Government legislation had previously made African Americans feel less than human . . . . there was the Missouri Compromise that basically gave states north of the Louisiana Territory the right to free slaves; the Dred Scott Decision that denied slaves citizenship and gave whites the right to return refugee slaves (and free black people) to the South—Georgia, South Carolina, North Carolina, and other Southern territories with no legal recourse; and finally the Emancipation Proclamation that declared freedom for slaves. But it was not until after the Civil War that slaves were truly emancipated in the South. And the sharecropping process, which was prevalently used in the South, was in effect a type of slavery; black people worked on white farms to produce and harvest crops for which they only received a portion of the profit from sales. The landowner received the other portion as "rent".

Georgia, like many states in the South, was known for its inhumane treatment of slaves. According to Mortimer Thomson, a reporter for the *New York Tribune*, the "largest sale of human beings in the history of the United States" took place at a racetrack in Savannah, Georgia in March of 1857 when Pierce Butler, a prominent, wealthy Philadelphian, sold 436 of his slaves to prevent personal bankruptcy. African Americans were sold as "property" to the highest bidder. Thomson wrote in his "What Became of Slaves on a Georgia Plantation": "On the faces of all was an expression of heavy grief; some appeared to be resigned to the hard stroke of Fortune that had torn them from their homes, and were sadly trying to make the best of it; some sat brooding moodily over their sorrow, their chins resting on their hands, their eyes staring vacantly, and their bodies rocking to and fro, with a restless motion that was never stilled". Savannah would always be referred to with disdain by blacks and historians who referred to the incident as the *Weeping Time*.

Savannah was home to many Negroes or coloreds, as black folk were called in that day. Mammy, as we affectionately called my grandmother, moved to Savannah when I was young. It is not known for sure but it is almost certain that she was the child of slaves. Mammy was a handsome coal black woman who had grown up in Millen, Georgia. On March 12th, 1890, she gave birth to a son whose father was a white man. Her son and my father, James (Jim) Clark, grew to become a very handsome mulatto young man. Mammy and her white companion made sure that James Clark was educated; he knew how to read, write, and perform basic mathematical calculations. Because he was half white he was very aggressive and assertive. He had been born free; the idea of enslavement or inhibition was completely foreign to him. It was constantly instilled in him that a man's reach should exceed his grasp.

My Father had several young black women whom he courted. He believed in living life to the fullest and had never thought seriously about marrying any one of them until he met my Mother, Ina Mae Chandler. Ina was a beautiful bronze colored woman with a broad face and high cheekbones. Her hair was jet black; her eyes a beautiful light brown. While Dad's ancestry included a white man, Mom was part Indian. James and Ina fell in love and were married on July 24th, 1910. When Ina married James, she was already with child. Dad loved her anyway; it was agreed that the child would be given the Clark name and that my Dad would

PEGGIE WARD KOON, PH.D.

bring her up as his own. Later, at the right time, this child was told the truth about her parentage. She was even encouraged (and allowed) to visit her biological father and his family. You see, way back then, my parents were forward-thinking enough that they understood how important it would be for my sister to know her heritage.

The year, 1912, marked the beginning of a series of events in America and the world. It was a time of wealth when men felt that they were in total control of their destinies. By 1912, people believed they could fly in the air like birds; the Wright brothers had built several successful airplane models. Admiral Scott and his party successfully made it to Antarctica but died on their way back home only miles from the nearest outpost. The unthinkable happened in April of that year; the largest luxury cruise liner ever built, the Titanic, sank. The Olympics were held in Stockholm, Sweden. Bohr discovered his length calculation for the radius of positive sphere of the atom, which changed the way that the world studied atomic models. The Balkan Conflict began, which ultimately led to the first world conflict in Europe, World War I. The world was in a state of prosperity and flux.

While all of these things were happening in the world, James and Ina Clark celebrated the 4th of July with my birth; I was born just after midnight, early on July 5th, 1912 down in Screven County Georgia. They named me, their baby girl, Irene. Although I was their *second* child, I was special; I was Jim's first born. For as long as I lived I would be his baby— the apple of his eye. And as was expected I shared his mulatto good looks, and my Mother's black Indian hair and high cheekbones. Everyone said that I was beautiful!

As I look back on my life, I realize that my personality and temperament were reflective of the time during which I was born and lived. I have always been called beautiful, intelligent, strong, intuitive, aggressive, fearless, and inquisitive-traits, all of which were encouraged by my Father. And I always shared his eagerness to learn; my Dad taught me that I could rise as far as I could reach and even higher—that I was only limited by my own desire and the will of God.

My Dad was also prosperous during this time. As the old folks would say, "He had the favorable hand of God on his side". He rented property from old man Newton but he did not sharecrop. He paid the old man a set amount of monthly rent; what he grew and raised was his own to sell or to keep. He built a new house with a room for each of us girls. He farmed the land and had his own animals, crops, horses, buggies, mules, and everything. My Dad was the first black man in our little community to own a car and the only one with any formal education.

My Father understood the importance of an education since Mammy had never been allowed to learn to read or write. Mammy had told him of her plight and the plight of other black folks, who had been used by whites with more knowledge than the poor unsuspecting souls of whom they took advantage. Because Dad was half white and educated he had enjoyed an elevated status among both whites and blacks in this small rural area. Education had always given him an advantage in life; he was bound and determined that his children, and their children, and their children's children—for generations to come—would be equipped with the knowledge to rise above adversity. He became a member of the National Congress of Colored Parents and Teachers, a membership he used to actively participate in the education and training of his children. His last known membership was in 1958; he was 68.

While my Father instilled in all of us children his love for learning, he also made every effort to ensure that we loved God. Dad believed that God was the Creator and Maker of all things; he taught his children to revere and worship Him. In 1913, Dad and Mom were in the group of builders and founders of Dickey Grove Baptist Church; we were brought up in that Church. My Dad always said that people who

believe in God are not satisfied with themselves if they are
not in the Church. It is the place where you are sure to find
and communicate with Him. It is also the secret to bringing
up children. In the Church children learn to put God first.
They learn how to speak and what to speak about. It also
teaches them to use respectable words; you will find no curse
words in the Church. And it teaches them to love, honor,
and respect God, their parents, their elders, and themselves.
The Clark family believed that life should be full of hard
work and play; but we always made time for God.

My Dad cared about everything and took care of
everything. Although he probably had a Bible earlier in his
life (since often times black children were taught reading
and writing using the Bible stories as a foundation literary
work), we know that Dad bought a family bible, *Beautiful
Bible Stories*, by Rev. Jesse Lyman Hurlbut, D.D., on May 28th,
1914—just two years after I was born. Since there were no
formal records kept of his children's birth dates except for
the Census, Dad recorded each birth (and death) of his
children, grandchildren, and their spouses in this Bible. The
Bible was not only a source of beautiful inspirational stories
that helped motivate and encourage us, it was also our family's
book of records. In it he safely tucked addresses, postal
notices, and other important papers.

All throughout the Holy Bible there is an emphasis on
birth rite of the firstborn; favor was always given to that child.
The story of Abraham and Sarah, with Ishmael and Isaac,
emphasizes that while Abraham's firstborn was Ishmael the
birth rite belonged to Isaac, Abraham and Sarah's first born,
as heir to God's promise to Abraham. Isaac was blessed
because of his inheritance and his heritage. In many ways
my birth was similar; though I was not my Mother's first child
I was the firstborn of my Father and my Mother. And so as
the firstborn of their union I was born with a proverbial spoon
in my mouth and the special love of a Father, James Clark.

My name is Irene Clark. My Father, James Clark, was a proud and accomplished black man who taught all of his children by example. I adored him; I loved my Mother, too. But my life long aspiration was to live a life that would be pleasing to God and to my "Dad".

The First Meeting

"And Enoch walked with God", the preacher would say. How many times had I heard the preacher at Dickey Grove preach the sermon about the man who was translated, who was such a good servant, that he never died, but was taken up to heaven? So many that deep down in my heart, this kind of Godly man was the man that I prayed for. Ironically, both my sister and I would meet men from vastly different backgrounds who would have the servant's name, Enoch.

When I was about five years old I first met my future husband, Enoch Ward. As I recall the meeting I remember when a young boy who appeared to be much older came up to our house on a mule to borrow my Dad's buggy. My older sister and I were standing on the porch when the young boy arrived. "Evenin'!" the boy said. "Is your Pa home?". We giggled and then replied, "No, our Dad is gone". The boy's Father, Jim Ward, had sent young Enoch to borrow a buggy so that the family could go to Church. It was not uncommon for the black folks in the area to ask each other for help. And since my Dad owned cars, mules, horses, and buggies—several different modes of transportation—he would have gladly loaned the family the buggy had he been home. We children, however, would not dare loan or give our parents' buggy or even a cup of sugar without their approval. "All right", the boy said, as he got back on his mule and ever so slowly went down the road. My sister caught the boy staring back at me from a distance. Enoch later confided in me that from the first time he saw me he thought I was the most beautiful little girl he had ever seen. Later he would admit that he was determined that he would marry me some day.

As for me, well I was too young (Enoch was 6 years older) at heart to worry about such things. "I think he likes you", my sister chided. "Hog wash!" I said, as we ran off to play. This was the first of many times that I would see the boy named Enoch Ward in passing. I did not realize it then but God arranged that meeting; I was going to spend the better years of my life with this boy. And what made it so wonderful, we did not have to learn to love each other after we married because we grew up together; we already loved each other. But for then he was just another boy, one of many who would later come to court one of the famous "Clark" girls of Screven County.

For the next few years I saw Enoch almost every day. While my Dad insisted that getting an education be the first priority for his children, the Ward boys made working in the fields their first order of business; their Father died when they were still young and the family depended on them in order to survive. The school was a mile or so up from where we lived so we left home early in the morning before daybreak to arrive on time. There were no clocks; the cock would crow and the sunshine would begin to beam on our faces through the window. A typical school day began with my Mom calling us to get out of bed; we would hit the floor running. We would take turns washing in a washbasin. Baking soda was a staple for underarms, brushing teeth, and all sorts of things. After washing up we would get dressed and Mom would comb our hair. We would have grits and eggs, warm hot biscuits made from homemade buttermilk and churned butter and Grandmother's fresh cane syrup or Mom's preserves. Then we were off to school!

Several of us (including the other black children in the area) would walk up the red clay dirt road to the one room school. This particular day like most days, the school bus carrying the white children would pass slowly by the other children and me. This day, however, was different. One of the white children on the bus looked back and yelled, "Hey, Niggers!" Most of the other black children had been conditioned to ignore such statements. They knew what retaliation might mean to them or their parents—but not me. I yelled just as boldly back, "Hey, Cracker!" The other children followed suit and yelled, "Yeah, Cracker". You know I smiled, thinking that my Father would be proud of my reaction to the slanderous name-calling. He had taught us about our heritage and the subjugated position of black people. He had also drilled in us that we should not be subservient followers who were afraid to fight for our God given rights; and he had promised us that he would always be there to support us in our time of need. We all believed in and lived by the principles our Father taught us; my bold steadfast approach to life was evidence that he had succeeded in making me, his first-born child, a leader.

When my older sister and I came home from school that day, my Father called us one by one to his side to tell him what we had learned. My older sister was called first. Bless her heart, she was always a socialite; she was very pretty and loved to have conversations with the other children. She could tell Dad everything that the other children overheard their parents talk about and all of the latest gossip. To his disappointment she could remember very little about the lessons of the day. It was not that she was incapable of learning; in fact I always thought my sister was very smart. As I recall how we were educated, she was probably bored and was not concerned enough to ask for more challenging work. Since children of all age groups were in the same classroom with one teacher, each child had to become responsible to some degree for the learning process. Those who desired to learn more had to *push* the teacher to obtain the individual attention that was required to continually advance.

"That's not what I meant; I meant what did you learn from the teacher!" Dad would say; "Did you have any homework?" "Yes Sir", she would reply. "Well then at least go do that, please", he'd say, shaking his head and smiling. He did not get angry because he understood that each of us had different aspirations and he encouraged that individuality. "Okay Renie, come here and tell Daddy what you learned today", he would say with affectionate anticipation. Dad knew that I was not only very smart but also aggressive. You see my Father was my role model; I had watched him achieve repeated successes as he paid close attention to every detail. I am so glad that I inherited this trait as well. Without hesitation I would recite poems, multiplication tables, read a verse, and repeat the entire group of lessons learned flawlessly. My memory was photographic although it would be much later before anyone actually recognized this character trait in me. When I finished my recitation Dad would give me a big kiss on the cheek and say, "That's my girl. Irene, knowledge is power." "Don't ever stop learning. I'm so proud of you", he would say. My Mother, though standing quietly in the background, also gave me an affirming smile of approval. Our family was very affectionate; I would reach over and give my Dad a big hug and a kiss and say, "I love you Dad. I'm going to go and finish my homework!" I did not bother to tell him about the incident with the white children on the bus; my big sister had already filled him in on all of the details.

At this early stage in my life I had already begun to realize the important role that parents play in a child's life. Even way back then, I noticed that my parents were different. While we were taught our proper "place" in the family we were also extended a level of respect for our own individual personalities and goals in life. As I grew older I also realized that while my parents had dreams and aspirations for each of us, they supported us in achieving goals that we set for ourselves. And if we made a mistake it was okay. My Dad would always say, *"You learn from your mistakes"*. The main thing to him was that we did *not* repeatedly make the same mistakes. We were also taught that we could always recover. The most important thing about falling was the getting back up! He taught us that cream always rises to the top and we were the cream!

My parents made our home a safe-haven to which we could always return. They were always there reinforcing, reaffirming, encouraging, and loving us as we each pursued our particular goals in life. In later years when I was allowed to visit the homes of other black children I began to truly appreciate how very special and formative my childhood relationships with my parents and siblings were in my development. I promised myself that when I had children I would share those experiences in an effort to create that same loving and supportive environment for them. Little did I know that I would nurture a group of ten children, who would excel beyond any measure my Father could have ever imagined. I have thought over and over again, "Oh, if only my Dad and Mom could see me now!"

The Baptism

Close your eyes and picture a lake or stream with cool water and black children dressed in white gowns with white cloths wrapped around their heads. A black man in a white pastor's robe is standing in knee—deep water while black men and women surround the edge of the water singing: *"Take me to the water, take me to the water, take me to the water to be baptized; none but the righteous, none but the righteous, none but the righteous, shall be saved"*. I can hear them singing that song and the voice of the Baptist preacher as he recites the words: "I now baptize you in the name of the Father, the Son, and the Holy Ghost" as the child is dipped into the cool water, eyes closed, breath held, waiting for the longest minute in life to pass. Up out of the water the child takes a gasp of fresh air—the song begins again: *"I love Jesus, I love Jesus, I love Jesus, Yes I do"*.

"Did you see that?", one of the little old ladies would say. "Too young; she ain't got nothin' yet; should'na been baptized!", the little old woman would go on and on gossiping with one of the other sisters. That's exactly what happened to many a young black child in the South. Baptism was a statement—not just an act. It was an acknowledgement to all who watched the ritual of the ceremony, that the child had reached the age at which s/he was now responsible to God for his/her actions. The baptized child was expected to understand that "the wages of sin is death" and that s/he is "saved by the grace of God". The child must know in his/her heart that Jesus Christ died for his/her sins. It was a serious matter that included both the *confession* of sin and the *profession* of faith. And no child was ever baptized if it was not believed that the child was "ready" for the baptismal process.

Now, I had watched these ceremonies time and time again. And I had heard my Mother and Father pray and confess their faith in God and Jesus Christ; I knew that nothing would please my Father more than my baptism. He had always taught us that while he enjoyed living here on earth, his greatest desire was to meet Jesus—and he wanted all of us to be there in heaven together on that "*Great Day*". I did not understand the true meaning of my Father's words because I could not visualize or "*see*" God; I believed in Him even loved Him but I could not see Him. But then I *saw* a lot of different things in my young life, many of which it would be much later before I understood.

My Mother, Ina Clark, was a housemaid for a white family while Dad worked on his own farm. Dad prided himself in the fact that although he had many children, with hard work and determination he had been able to provide his family with as much as if not more than most of his black neighbors and some of the white ones, too! And he was proud of his freedom and his heritage; he was not afraid to tell any man, white or black, what he felt. He refused to be just another sharecropper; and with that refusal was an even greater disdain for subservience. When my Mother would ask him why he would not go to work for the man for whom she worked my Dad would say, "Now why would I want to work for him, Ina?" "Why, he barely has as much as we do; he's just another common man—like me. If I was going to work for somebody it would be someone who had more than me; someone who could help me to better myself." Although my Dad meant every word he said he really meant no disrespect for the white man; he was just stating the facts. He truly believed that a person should constantly strive to better himself. This kind of verbiage or "*talk*" was often misconstrued by both blacks and whites as displaying disrespectful arrogance.

In those days Southern white gentlemen feared such an educated black man. Any black person who stood up for his beliefs was considered arrogant, needing to be taught a lesson. Now I always heard everything; I watched every move that my Dad made. One night when it was pitch dark I saw men in white robes come to our house—not the kind that I saw at the baptismal ceremony but the hooded kind that are used to hide the face of the wearer. These men came for my Dad; they called for him, "Come on out, Jim!". He was not afraid; he walked outside to meet them. I peered through the window afraid to breathe—frightened at the thought of what might happen, as they took my Dad away. I overheard my Mother and others later say that those men beat him because he was considered a boasting "nigger"—a nonconformist. That night when Dad returned home I heard him tell Mom that he had been given an ultimatum—"Leave now!" My Dad had been exiled from our home. He thought all of his children were asleep—and all of them were except me! I saw Dad when he came back all beaten up; I cried but not loudly enough to be heard. I would have been punished if Mom and Dad discovered that I was eavesdropping because children were not allowed to meddle in the business of grown folks. Anyway, I sneaked back into my bed; the next morning Mom told us that Dad had gone to Savannah to work for a while. The truth was that my Dad had been forced to flee—back to his beloved Mother in Savannah for refuge.

During the next several months my sisters, brothers and I would visit our Dad in Savannah along-with my Mother. At one point Mother actually moved all of us to Savannah to be with Dad. She found it difficult to stay away from the country that she loved so much—the people, the way of life—she could not adjust to the city. And so she moved us all back to her home and resumed working for the same white man as a housekeeper. In the meantime, Dad worked for the shipyard in Savannah. He would travel back and forth between our home and Savannah, spending as much time as possible with my Mother and all of us children, being careful not to be seen by the men in white.

My Mother would cry constantly; she missed my Dad so much. She had never known the identity of the men who beat her husband because their faces were hidden; but she suspected all along that it might be the man for whom she worked. He was always fond of her; she was a beautiful black woman who was respectful and loyal. Daily the man watched her, crying as she worked diligently to complete the cleaning and washing she had been given. Finally he approached her, "Ina, why are you crying", he'd say. "It's nothing", she would reply. "Is it Jim? Do you miss him that much?", he would query. Still Mother would give no reply. "All right, if it will put a smile on your face and stop you from crying you can tell him that he can come back. But he'll have to stay in his place and watch his mouth!". "You hear me? Tell him he can come back but he'd better watch his step!", he said. "Yes, sir", she said. The Clarks believed in the importance of family. They had all been taught to take care of each other no matter what. It had been several months since my Dad had lived at home; so all of us were elated when our Dad returned. It was a time for celebration. Life would finally be back to normal for a while; however it would be years before Dad would move back into our home permanently.

We had no toilets except for the wooden out houses that were built in the back of the house; the Clark outhouses had two seats. My big sister and I would always arrange to "go" at the same time; neither of us was especially fond of

going to the outhouse alone. "I'm so sick; I believe that I'll
have to go in the hospital when I get older", my sister said.
"Why?" I asked. "I don't know I just feel it", she replied. I
loved my sister so much; I wanted nothing but the best for
us both. We were only a year apart and we did almost
everything together; we were very close. I could not bear
the thought that something bad might happen to her; I always
tried to reassure her. "Don't say that; you'll get better", I
would say in a calm voice. You see even back then my faith
was so strong; I believed as I do now that all things are possible
through God. I prayed daily that my Dad would come home
and God had answered my prayers so I knew that God could
heal any sickness my sister had, too. And because of this faith
I was determined that I was ready to be baptized.

It was May of 19 and 19; I wasn't quite 7 years old when
my parents let my sister and me spend the week with
Mammy. Mammy took us with her to a revival at Rock Hill
Baptist Church. I remember hearing the eloquent voice of
the pastor, Rev. Berrien, under the revival tent calling all
sinners to Christ. I recall vividly how Rev. Berrien's voice
resounded back in those days. There were no microphones,
speakers, or pianos. The people just sang from the bottoms
of their hearts. You could hear them singing, "Free at Last,
Free at Last. Thank God Almighty, I'm Free at Last". You
could hear them for miles before you ever reached the tent,
singing like voices from heaven. As a child the distance
seemed so far back then when in reality we had only walked
about a mile or two to the tent. Oh how they sang!

When the preacher called for sinners I felt something
come over me; I did not understand it then but it was the
Holy Spirit. I could not sit still; I jumped up and before I
knew it I had given the preacher my hand. That night I gave
my heart to Christ. That was in May of 1919. All of us who
joined the Church during the revival were scheduled to be
baptized that following Sunday morning—bright and early
at the pond nearby. When my Mother came to get us that

Saturday Mammy told her that I was going to be baptized. I never will forget it; my Mother looked at me sternly and said, "No. Irene, you ain't got nothin' yet; you too young! I don't wanna hear no mo 'bout it! You too young!" In those days children respected and obeyed their parents. Even though my faith was real I decided to be obedient and wait until God softened my Mother's heart. I prayed to God constantly asking Him to change her mind and He did.

In August of that year I went to a revival with my Mother at our Church, Dickey Grove Baptist Church. Oh, how Rev. Ike Washington could preach, pray, and sing! This time I would join; when he called it was as if God Himself had called out to me. Again, I could feel the presence of the Holy Spirit and I could not sit still! I walked swiftly down to meet him, gave the preacher my hand, and professed my belief in God and my savior, Jesus Christ. I've been serving Him ever since that day! My Mother did not want me to join the first time; but the second time she *saw* the Spirit move in me and allowed me to join. God answered my prayers. Reverend Ike Washington baptized me, Irene Clark, at Dickey Grove Baptist Church in August of 1919.

By the time I was 10 years old I had begun composing papers for girls to read at Church anniversaries. I started reading my own Church's History at Dickey Grove Baptist Church's anniversary. My parents were proud of me; and I was just as proud as I am now to work and serve God in the Church. I felt so blessed. What was so thrilling about it was that I was born in 1912 and the Church was built in 1913. I grew up *with and in* the Church; as I stood up each year to read the Church's History it was like reading about a part of my own life! At an early age I began a circle of influence within the Church that in the years to come would be expanded farther than I could have ever fathomed.

The Courtship

The *Clark girls,* as we were called, had a reputation in the County for our beauty and intelligence. We were also not shy or "bashful" as the old folks would call it in those days. Dad and Mom believed in working and playing hard. They instilled in all of us the value of hard work; but they insisted that we spend ample time enjoying the finer things in life. They did not believe in keeping us shut up in a house; they wanted us to go out and see the world. Many of the Negro girls in that day were not allowed to go out on dates. Since Mom and Dad were frequently out with other adults frolicking, they had no problems if we did the same. We learned at an early age "to carry ourselves in a respectful manner"; besides, no boy would ever dare try to take advantage of one of my Dad's daughters. We were beauties and our father's pride and joy; any boy who even attempted to take advantage of one of us would pay dearly. The local boys knew that; and so did the girls. The Clark girls were the envy of every black girl in the area.

During the week, all of us attended a one-room school and all of us worked. There were hours set aside for learning, working, and plenty of time for play—especially on the weekends. As young girls and boys we all looked forward to the weekend, just as young people do today. It is amazing to me how some parents are unable to empathize with their children; as old as I am, I can remember how important it was to be able to go out and have fun with young people my age. I also remember how important it was to be properly dressed and groomed for the occasion. My parents recognized that, too. They made every effort to ensure that we were ready in every respect to interact successfully with our peers in a social setting. Now on occasion some young boys would come from neighboring communities to a party or to court a young girl. Peter Roberts was one such boy from Sylvania. He was wild and handsome; several of the girls had a crush on him. But he had his eye on me.

On the weekends it was not uncommon for all of us Clark children who were *of age* to go to town to parties. Most of the time my big sister and I would go to the parties together. These parties were held in big open rooms with tables where you could buy snacks and non-alcoholic drinks—similar to hors d'oeuvres and punch that are served at social gatherings today. There would be people playing music—a band of sorts—and a dance floor. Not many of the girls in the area knew how to dance; our parents had made sure that we were taught ballroom and social dances. I knew the waltz, the jig, and the fox trot.

When we walked into the room the boys and girls would all turn around and stare. We usually were the best-dressed and best-looking girls in the place—so we were told. Almost always the Ward boys, James and Enoch, would be the first to approach us. They were such gentlemen; they would politely offer to buy us something to eat or drink. My sister, who always loved to eat, would never refuse. The Ward boys didn't know how to dance; so other boys would ask us and we would leave James and Enoch to go out onto the dance floor. My sister thought it was funny to allow the Ward boys to buy us food and sodas and then go dance with other boys at the party; I always felt awkward accepting their treats. However, we had been taught it was rude and impolite to refuse. Out of respect we would return to talk to the Ward boys after each dance.

At the end of the party one evening Peter Roberts grabbed me and asked if he could give me a ride home. "What about my sister?", I asked. "Oh, she can come, too!", Peter replied. There was just one problem—the buggy that was drawn by a beautiful white horse could only seat two comfortably. "I know what we'll do!", I laughed. I told my sister to sit in the seat next to Peter; I would ride home on Peter's lap! It was considered outrageous! I was the talk of the town, especially at the Ward household. Hattie, Enoch's Mother, knew that her son was hopelessly in love with me. "I don't see why any one would want to marry a girl like that!" she exclaimed. The Ward girls, on the other hand, admired my daring. As for Enoch, he had been hit by cupid; there was no hope. He would later tell me that I was the girl of his dreams; after that night he was determined to make me his wife.

Of course Peter Roberts took my gesture as a first step in what he had hoped would lead to romance, while I thought nothing of the whole incident; it was just a ride home. I just did what was practical to get us home. When Peter came to call on me I feigned sleep. In my heart I secretly admired Enoch. On the other hand, my Father disapproved of the boy saying that he was too old and accomplished with women for his daughter. In reality James Clark did not believe that any man was suitable for his beloved Irene.

Just as my Dad and Mom had helped to build Dickey Grove Baptist Church, Enoch's parents, James and Hattie Ward, had helped to build Rockyford Baptist Church. We were both very proud of our parents' involvement in the building of these two prominent churches in the area. Enoch had decided to call on me and so he invited me on our first date. He asked me to go with him to his family's Church and

I agreed. I recall that I got up early that Sunday morning and bathed, put on a brand new Sunday dress and shoes, and combed my long, black hair. While Enoch was helping me into the buggy my Father had sneaked out back. Dad did not trust Enoch and had decided to follow just slightly behind us all the way to make sure that the boy did not try anything with me.

Shortly after we arrived in the churchyard Dad appeared. After the service I went up to my Father and said, "Dad, I didn't know you were coming to Rockyford today?" Dad looked at me smiling apologetically and said, "I didn't believe that boy was really bringing you to Church. I wanted to make sure that you were okay, Renie". He looked at me affectionately; "I'm sorry." I wasn't angry at Dad for following me; in fact I was so grateful that he cared that much about me that I reached over and hugged and kissed my Father and said, "It's okay. I love you, Dad". My Dad made sure that I knew how much I meant to him; and it was because of his attentiveness and affection for me that I loved him so much.

When I think about that day and look at how some people just throw away their kids today, it really makes me sad. Because as tough as times were back then, and they were tough, my parents and others cared for and looked after the welfare of their children. I always taught my own children how important it is to show others how much you care for your family; it helps them to treat them and you better. My Father taught me to demonstrate my love for others through actions not just words, a rule I have lived by throughout my entire life.

The whole Church, including Enoch Ward, knew how much my Dad, James Clark, loved me, his daughter Irene. They *observed* the meaning of a protective, loving, Father. And Enoch knew that he would have to earn Dad's trust before he would ever be able to marry me. As the years went by my Dad would learn to trust, respect, and yes, even love Enoch. Those years were yet to come. In the meantime, my

Dad would watch Enoch like a hawk every step of the way as he properly courted his Renie.

During the next several months I was courted by a couple of the local young men, including Enoch. My younger sister had already married. One of my suitors asked me to marry him; even though I really loved Enoch, I felt obliged to marry the man because of my age. You see at 16 a girl was considered an old maid if she had not married; so I decided that I would accept the proposal. In my heart I truly felt that it was time for me to wed. However, in those days parental consent was obtained before the young man was given a definite answer. When I told my Mother she cried hysterically, refusing to stop until I agreed to refuse the proposal. It was the oldest manipulative trick in the book and I knew that my Mother was faking; nevertheless, I complied with my Mother's request. During this time my older sister met a young man named Enoch, whose parents owned land, cattle, chicken, crops, and horses. He asked for her hand in marriage; Dad was well pleased with her choice of husband and after a proper courtship agreed to allow the two to marry. I was lost without my big sister; we had always been inseparable. Now throughout this entire time, Enoch never stopped *calling on* me. Although I dated him from time to time, my very first priority became finishing my education.

In May, of 1931 at the age of 18 I finished school as far as we (black folks) could go in that little area back then. I was very proud that I had completed my education; my Dad was also very pleased. At the age of 18 I wanted to get married; my Mother wanted nothing more than for me to find a good man to wed. The primary reason that a mother wanted her daughter to find a good man was to make sure that she would be cared for; a Father wanted his son to marry to carry on the family name. It was a tradition—when a woman came of age, she was expected to marry. So when Enoch proposed to me I immediately agreed. He then followed proper protocol and asked my Father for my hand in marriage.

Dad called me into the other room to talk to me. "Renie, you know that I love you and I want you to be happy", he said. "Yes, Dad", I said, nodding with understanding. James Clark went on to explain that the man who was asking for my hand in marriage was too old (Enoch was 6 years older than me). He then explained how Enoch had dated all of these other women, some of whom were married. I just listened but did not waiver. Finally he said, "He has nothing! Where will you live?" By this time I knew that my Father was desperate; Dad had never been one to worry about the welfare of any of his children. He had always taught us that God would provide. I just looked at him and smiled. "Dad, I'm going to marry him. We'll be fine. It's okay. Now go on back in there and tell him he can have my hand in marriage". "But Renie", he said. I kissed him on the cheek and he begrudgingly gave Enoch his permission to marry me, his favorite daughter. On reflection I realized no man would have ever been "good enough" for me; this was one decision that I could not have ever allowed my Father to make!

On the first Sunday in June of 1931 Irene Clark, the *second* daughter of James and Ina Clark, and Enoch Ward, the second son of Jim and Hattie Ward, were married. It was a simple wedding at my parents' house. Enoch's brother, James, was his best man; my best friend, Sophie, was my bridesmaid. Enoch had been working and was almost late for the ceremony; he had put his wedding suit on top of his work clothes because he had not had time to change. When the preacher pronounced us man and wife I leaned over to kiss my new husband. I felt the suspenders of his overhaul pants beneath Enoch's shirt. "Oh God, what have I done?" I thought. In my mind I remembered all of the years that I had known Enoch and his family; we had so much in common, especially our love for God. And yet for that one moment I wondered about the strange man that I had married—a man about which I thought I knew everything but really knew very little; a man who had not taken the time to change clothes and clean up before our wedding. Little did I know that Enoch had been working that day to help a friend who had given us a wood—burning stove for our new home. He wanted only the best for me and he was determined that he would do everything in his power to provide for me in the manner in which I was accustomed.

We spent our wedding night at his Mother's house. After the wedding we lived in a small house on Mr. Ned's place (Ned was a white man for whom Enoch worked). The next day we would begin a long journey as a couple in a labor of love that would endure for over 60 years!

By the Numbers

Have you ever read the book of Numbers in the Holy Bible? Well I thought I would never have children; instead I realized that I had inherited my Mother's ability to procreate. My Mother, Ina Clark, would have a total of 17 children of which 14 lived. Of the 14 that lived, each would have their fair share of offspring. I would have eleven-five boys and six girls. I would lose my second girl in death—a death that was recorded in Jim Clark's Bible for all posterity. The family tree could be written in later years like the book of Numbers . . . And James and Ina begat Irene who married Enoch; Enoch and Irene begat James Earl who married Thelma; James and Thelma begat, Edwina, who married Dominic; Dominic and Edwina begat Jasmine who begat . . . , etc., and so on and so on. It is truly amazing to look at the Clark family tree, which when drawn in a chart on paper covers an entire wall! By the numbers the Clark family tree is large.

For now though we will go back in time to 1931. The first thing that I did was to change my membership from Dickey Grove Baptist Church to his Church, Rockyford Baptist Church. I remembered the passage from the Book of Ruth that says, "*Thy people shall be my people*". Oh what a lovely biblical testimony for married couples! The members at Rockyford Baptist Church welcomed me into their fold since it was understood that a good Christian woman should follow her husband to his place of worship. And I was not a pew warmer; I immediately began working in the Church and made it my own! Months passed and although Enoch and I tried, I could not conceive. Enoch and I worked and played hard. Of course I was content being a housewife; Enoch took care of everything. He treated me like a queen; I only worked if and when I wanted to. The other black women would look at me with jealousy and envy. If Mister Ned came to my house and asked, "Irene, why ain't you out there in the fields?" I would assertively reply, "Because I don't feel like it! I am going to wash and clean up my house today. Now, you have a good day!" Mister Ned loved me like a daughter; as the years went by he would affectionately refer to me as his "baby girl". He would come and sit down and have a glass of ice water or ice tea with me; we would chat for hours about the hard times that they were going through, while the rest of the black women worked in the fields. "The pressure is on, real bad', I would hear him and the other older folks say. This expression referred to the depression era that existed in the United States at that time.

It was probably the worst time in the world for two people to get married. Herbert Hoover was president and the depression, which began with *Black Tuesday* in 1929, was still in full swing. Food and clothing were rationed. It didn't matter how much money you had you could only buy so much flour, sugar, salt, pepper, rice, baking soda, and other staples. Those of us on the farm could at least eat what we grew. Times were really tough—not just for blacks, but for everyone. The crash of the Stock Market and the subsequent removal of money from banks by those who watched large financial institutions go bankrupt caused some folks to lose all faith in the American government and its institutions. As people leaped from buildings to their death, my Dad would refer to them as "fools". He could not rationalize or see the logic behind such drastic measures over money. But then although my Dad saved money for hard times, he had not invested his life savings in the stock market. What he did have he shared with the less fortunate. And he never lost faith in the fact that God would provide. I watched my Father live successfully through the depression by remembering these basic principles; with great conviction I adopted them as my own. And to this day I keep 20 pounds of sugar, flour, salt, meal, and other staples on hand in my cupboard—just in case!

When Enoch and I started out I coerced Enoch to ask his Mother for his bed. She refused. "Enoch, you are young; I am old", Hattie Ward sternly told her son. "When you decided to take a wife you took on the responsibility of a grown man. It is now your responsibility to provide for her, not mine. Go out and work and buy a bed for the two of you to sleep on or cut down some trees and make one! But you can't have mine!" I was always one to pay attention to actions and words; I heard every word loud and clear. I had heard the whispers and gossip when I accompanied Enoch to Church on our first date; the Ward family had not forgotten the tale of the brash little girl who yelled "Cracker" back at the white boy on the bus. They had also not forgotten the brazen girl who sat in Peter Roberts' lap all the way home from a dance at night. There was also envy; I was continually referred to as *pretty*; I had a glowing light brown complexion with light brown eyes and jet black hair—what black folk called *good hair*. I stood 5 feet 4 inches tall and weighed 125 pounds; with a figure like a Coca-Cola bottle I was said to be "*tailor made*". Many of the black folk in the community perceived that the Clarks thought they were "*better*" than others. We were not taught that we were "better" than others; but we were brought up with very high levels of self-esteem and pride. Ours was a very positive upbringing that was filled with faith in God, encouragement, and hope—even in the most desperate of times.

Few people took the time to know my heart; my so-called *good looks* were coupled with an aggressive high-strung personality that was tempered by an inherently good nature. Nevertheless, I was often characterized as bold, cocky, boastful, and quick to speak my mind—qualities that Hattie and many of the other black women in the rural area deemed inappropriate for a *respectable* woman. I cried at the thought that for these reasons Hattie had denied my new husband the use of the family's spare bed. Later I would begin to understand and agree with her stance. She was an older widow who could not work or build things. She would probably not be able to easily replace the bed if she needed it later on. We were young and were able to sleep on the floor if necessary until we got what we needed. It was a valuable lesson for us both, one that I would not forget. In later years *Enoch's Mother*, as I would always call her, was very kind to my children and me and I returned the kindness in every way possible.

My Father had taught us not to give up; if one approach failed we were told to try another. Remembering his words I dried my tears as I heard Enoch come down the hall to the room where we slept. I rallied my strength of character and said reassuringly to him, "Don't worry, Enoch. It'll be all right; I'll ask my Mother for my bed." When I went to my Mother and asked for my bed, she immediately agreed to give the bed to the two of us along-with a box for sitting. See the difference; my Mother was not using the bed and she knew we needed it so she freely gave it to us. It reminds me of the biblical passage that says that God loves a cheerful giver. This was yet another opportunity for Enoch to see how much my parents loved me.

Anyway, Enoch cut down some trees and took limbs and boards to make a table so that we could sit and eat. Every day my white girl friend, Louise, and I walked a mile to pick cotton in the fields; I picked enough cotton to make $2.00 and bought 2 chairs (for a dollar each). I cooked our food on that old wood-burning stove (the one Enoch worked for on the day of our wedding). There were many days that we only had bread and water but we were in love and happy.

Enoch would almost never want to pick the cotton; he felt he could earn more money chipping boxes. Even after we had cotton crops on our farm, he would rarely pick it; he thought it paid far too little for the work involved. I had to figure out ways to make him *want* to do the work to get him to help me pick it. I remembered how my Mother would use various tactics to get her way; I learned to use Enoch's innate desire to succeed to encourage him to accomplish things he would not otherwise have ever achieved. Some might call it *manipulation;* I would prefer to call it *motivation.* Whatever the term, I used this method to repeatedly accomplish our goals. Back then I would bet him that I could pick as much cotton as he could faster. Both of us had a competitive spirit and both wanted to win; our competition kept us going for several hours. We agreed to stop after we picked a thousand pounds. You would only get 25¢ per 100 pounds of cotton. The day's work would yield $2.50 each; together we had $5.00, which was quite a bit of money for a black or white person back then. I can never remember who actually finished first; I think I beat him! I always smile at the thought of winning. We'd take our money and go to town (Millen) to shop and buy things for our home and ourselves.

After what seemed an eternity I finally got pregnant (It really wasn't that long—a couple of months, but to me it seemed like forever). On July 15, 1932 our first son, James Earl Ward, was born. He looked just like my Dad and he had inherited most of my traits—good looks, bold, arrogant, and fearlessly determined! J.E., as he was affectionately called, was indeed a strong-willed child. This first born would be given every thing that he needed and more—all that the new Ward family could afford. We were both so proud that

I had given birth to this handsome little boy; we carried him with us everywhere so that all of those who thought I would be barren could see the beautiful baby boy that the Lord had given us.

James Earl Ward had been given a first name that honored both of his grandfathers; I could boast that he was named after my Dad and Enoch could say that he named him after his Father. The child would reap the benefits of an upbringing by parents from two vastly different yet very similar backgrounds. On the one hand, I was usually referred to as intelligent, hard working, beautiful, and courageous; on the other hand Enoch was called humble, hardworking, tall, and handsome. Both of us feared and loved God, both were honest, respectful, and competitive. James, our first-born, would inherit all of these qualities and more. He was charming and fun loving; J.E. would always be a *joy* to be around.

The country had a new president, Franklin Delano Roosevelt; his *New Deal* had just begun. There were still repercussions from the depression, though. And in 1933 the jobless rate for whites (not to mention blacks) was still high. Farmers had gotten some relief from legislation passed by the new president; the US economy was slowly but surely turning around. Enoch and I had moved onto Fred Chance's place, (not far from where his Mother lived), in a house with more room for our expanding family. By now through hard work and determination, we had begun to accumulate the things that were needed to *keep house*. People always told me that I had a green thumb. Back then you didn't have to do much as far as fertilizing the soil; it was already rich and full of nutrients. I had lovely flowers and a big beautiful garden with tomatoes, peppers, greens, peas, squash, and beets; we had chickens, cows, and plenty of land. We also planted soybeans, peanuts, and some corn; we gave Fred half of what we made on the sale of these crops as payment for the use of his land.

Enoch also sold turpentine; he had always been industrious so he would get up early in the morning before dawn to chip boxes. He enjoyed hunting; our hunting dogs were also pets. I loved to make a meal of fried rabbit with gravy and biscuits and fresh greens, corn, and tomatoes from the garden. It was a time when we rarely went hungry—very different from our first beginnings. God had truly blessed us; and Enoch had kept faith and determination that he would prove my Dad wrong. He would show his Father-in-law that he was more than capable of providing for me; he was committed to work as long and as hard as necessary to give me, his beloved wife Irene, all that I could ever want or need.

Enoch was a part of Fred Chance's extended family. Fred found him to be trustworthy, loyal, humble, and hardworking, an exemplary black man. Fred loved Enoch and me so much that he naturally loved our first-born child, James, too. When J.E. was 14, Fred pulled some strings to get a drivers license for him (even though he was under age), right along with his own boys. And although each one of my children had a special place in my heart, just as my parents had loved all 17 of their children, little James was special. Like my Father before me I always had a special place in my heart for my first-born.

Early in November of 1933 our second child, Charles Matthew, was born. Charles was also a handsome boy who was very welcomed into the family. James was so possessive of the new baby that he did not want him to be touched by anyone outside of the immediate family. Charles was quiet and humble, character traits inherited from Enoch. He was obedient and yet he had James Clark's daring desire for adventure. From the time he was born I knew he would be blessed and be a blessing. I tell him that continually to this day because he is always doing something for someone else. In those days it was usually James' chores that he would make sure were done; and although James thought he was taking advantage of his little brother it was his little brother Charles, who would benefit from the process. You see that is exactly what happens when you try to take advantage of another person's kindness. That person is the one who will get his just reward; and you—well you will most likely sit by the way side and watch as they just pass you by on the road to success. Charles saw what some would call adversity as an opportunity. Charles' hard work paid off; I knew he would be successful but I did not realize that he would emerge as the family's pioneer, moving us away from the farm—an act that would ultimately change the future of the entire family!

Almost two years passed before the third child was born. In May of 1935 Enoch and I were blessed with the arrival of little Lee Mark. My Father had always taught me that a child's name should have some meaning; he believed that as the child grew he or she would take on the characteristics and personality that were defined by that name. Enoch and I selected each child's first and middle name with careful thoughtfulness. I remembered the stories of the disciples (in the Bible) that my Dad had read to me as a child and deliberately named each of my boys after a biblical disciple. The middle name was especially important to me since neither of us had been given middle names by our parents. Perhaps this too was a subconscious method of allowing my children yet another choice; if the child did not like the first name s/he could always use the second. But of primary importance in my mind was making sure that there was some biblical reference in their names—a reminder that God should be first and foremost in their lives.

Dad seemed to play with little Lee Mark more than the other two boys. Perhaps it was because he was younger; but in retrospect I think that it was because he felt a special kindred with the boy. "Billy", as little Lee Mark would be later called, was very small in stature like his grandfather. Like Jim Clark he was full of life and mischief. By now the three children were a handful for me; James was three,

Charles was two, and Lee Mark was just a baby. On occasion Enoch's Mother would walk over to the house to help me with little Lee Mark; she would even take him home with her from time to time.

My days were spent as a full-time housewife and Mother. I cooked, washed clothes, cleaned and sewed for Enoch, the children, and me. I would make little garments and quilts by hand with thread and needle. My big sister would stop over and sometimes spend the night. And my Father came to see me at least once a week to make sure that Enoch treated me well. I seldom visited anyone because I did not ever go anywhere without my children; I spent time teaching them manners and reading to them. By the time they each reached the age of 3 or 4, I had taught them to pray at night:

> *"Now I lay me down to sleep, I pray the Lord my soul to keep.*
> *And if I should die before I wake, I pray to the Lord my soul*
>   *to take.*
> *God bless my Father, my Mother, my sisters, my brothers, and*
>   *me. Amen."*

You see I stayed home and trained my children while they were young, then when I took them out in public I was proud of the fact that I could look at my children and they understood by my expression that they should be careful; they were about to be spanked if they did not stop. I taught them to take care and to be careful; that is to say that I taught them to be careful with everything and to pay attention to every detail, overlook nothing. Now I felt truly blessed that the Lord had given me 3 healthy sons but I so wanted a little girl to dress up and call my own. I prayed and asked God to give me a little girl and in September of 1936, a little over a year after Lee Mark was born, I had my first girl. I named her *Annie* after my older sister and *Grace* because I felt that it was by the grace of God that my wish had been granted.

Grace was adorable; of course I said that about all of my

children. She had my complexion and long black hair. She was smart, a quick study, and always wanted to please her Mother. I took her everywhere; and because she was Enoch's first little girl she was also *"daddy's girl"*. This would prove to be a challenge for her as she approached the subject of marriage with her Dad, just as it had been for me with my Dad; no man would ever be good enough for Enoch's little *Grace*. The boys loved their little sister, too; but they also liked to pick at her. Grace was a tough little cookie, somewhat tom boyish in behavior. She was so very determined to be accepted by her brothers that she chipped in and often did more than her share of work and other chores around the house.

Grace was always aggressive. She would try anything! One afternoon after it had been raining, Enoch and I went out to get fodder for the horses and mules. J.E. decided to come along with us, leaving Charles to see after Lee Mark and Grace. Now while we were concentrating on gathering the fodder, we had completely forgotten about Charles, Lee Mark, and Grace. Charles and Lee Mark had walked down to the well, which was almost filled to the top with water from the rain. Grace, who wanted to be with her favorite brothers, went over to join them. When she finally got there Charles picked her up and lifted her above the well's wall so that her feet touched the water. Lee Mark and Charles repeated this little playful game, lifting her up in the air then lowering her until her little feet just barely touched the water—laughing the whole time. Grace laughed too, as she felt the cool water trickle across the bottom of heel down to her toes. Charles was young and had not considered that if she slipped out of his hands she would probably have drowned and died.

As we finished picking the fodder and I got closer to the house I saw Charles with Grace in his hands dipping her into the well. I did not dare startle him for fear that he would drop her. My heart raced as I walked ever so swiftly yet calmly toward them and grabbed her. When I had her firmly in my arms, I admonished Chuck for being so careless with his little sister. Little Lee Mark started crying; Grace didn't start crying until I started hugging and kissing her all over. Poor little thing, I guess she thought I was crazy! Anyway I scolded the boys, grabbed Lee Mark, and rocked him and Grace to sleep that night, grateful that the Lord had spared my child. I would tell this story to my children over and over again to help them understand how important it is for them to love and look after each other.

By 1938 I felt as if my family was complete. I had three sons and the daughter I had always wanted. Since there was no birth control women had children in God's time, not their own. I prayed and thanked God for my four children; at the same time I asked him to spare me from having any more. He did not answer my prayers—at least not the way I intended. That year on February 13th, Bernise was born. She was beautiful, more beautiful than all of my children. She was also a perfect baby in many respects; she did not cry very much and was just a joy to show off to neighbors, family, and friends.

It was the summer of the following year and Enoch had taken the car to town. Enoch had bought some canned berries so that I could make pies; blueberry cobblers were his favorite so I made one that afternoon just for him. The cobbler was still hot when I asked one of the boys to take the trash to the pile where it would be burned. Somehow one of the not quite empty blueberry cans fell on the ground near the back porch; I did not see it or I would have made the boys pick it up and carry it over to the trash pile out back.

A few days later the boys went outside to play in the yard just back of the house. Bernise was a little over a year old; the boys would often take her and Grace out onto the clear part of the yard to watch them as they played. I sat in a rocker on the back porch watching their every move to make sure they were okay. Back then we would fry cornbread in the skillet on top of the stove. I had some bread on top of the stove cooking and got up for no more than a minute to turn it over. When I returned I saw little Bernise with blueberries from the half-empty can all over her face. I ran and took the blueberry can away from her; I wiped my baby's mouth clean and gave her water to try and force the berries through her system. It was too late; my little girl had eaten too many of the berries that had been poisoned by the rusted can. Bernise developed a fever; the nearest doctor was miles away and Enoch was gone in the car. Since I could not drive I could not have taken the baby to the doctor even if the car had been at the house. I made a vow to myself that all of my children would learn how to drive!

Enoch did not know anything about Bernise's sickness; there were no phones so I could not reach him. He tarried in Millen drinking and talking with old friends. When he finally came home our baby was near death; we carried her on the long ride to the old country doctor's house but she died before she ever reached his office. Bernise died in June of 1939 and was buried at Dickey Grove Baptist Church. It was a traumatic time for our marriage. In fact for a long time I secretly hated Enoch and blamed him for our child's death. I cried out to God as I internalized the blame, thinking that God punished me because I asked him to stop me from having children. It was a hard lesson for me. Through Bernise's death I learned that we should be careful what we ask of God; he might answer our prayers in a totally different way than we desire. We should be thankful and grateful to God for everything. He knows best; we should let Him have His way in our lives. Oh how I cried out to Him in sorrow and repentance. And I cannot eat blueberries without remembering the death of my little girl; to this day I can barely eat them.

Despite my bitterness God did not frown on us through the years. He continually blessed our union. On February

12th in 1940 we had another little girl; Enoch named her Irene after his beloved *Renie*. It was as if subconsciously he named her after me to honor me—to say how sorry he was that we had lost our little girl. Although I loved this new addition to the family she would never replace my little Bernise. Doctors today say that whatever a woman does during her pregnancy affects the unborn child. I did not know this medically proven fact back then. And even if I had known it I am not sure that it would have changed the way I felt or behaved. I grieved for my Bernise so very much that my unborn baby's entire outlook on life was forever affected by my emotional state during that time. The first few years after her birth were hardly any better; little Irene grew up feeling as if she lived in someone's shadow. She would blame her older sister, Grace, for that "*feeling*" as she grew older. Irene was always striving to compete with Grace for my attention when in fact I treated her as if she was trying to fill the void created in me because of the loss of my Bernise. She could never be successful in winning my affection during this time since I was suffering from the worse kind of depression. Only God could fill the void in my heart left by Bernise's death.

As young Irene grew she resembled her Father in looks. Now remember that this was a time when I had only a bittersweet love for my husband, Enoch. It was a dark time in my life when I prayed constantly to God for forgiveness. I always wanted my children to feel loved and nurtured as I was as a child. I know it must have appeared to Irene that I doted all the more over Grace, paying her very little attention. I felt so helpless and Grace seemed to sense my loss, which made her all the more dear to me. I never lost my Faith in God; I sang and prayed, asking God for understanding. In time the Lord would show me His grace and mercy and I would understand it better by and by.

Augusta

On December 7, 1941, the Japanese attacked Pearl Harbor. World War II was beginning and the nation had been put on high alert that the Japanese were planning an invasion of America. Fred would give us his copy of the local paper and I would read it from front to back in an attempt to stay abreast of what was happening in the world; Enoch had bought a radio and the family sat around the living room to listen to FDR's fireside chats. Just as it is today, there were so many different stories of what was happening it was hard to distinguish truth from propaganda. I turned 30 years old on July 5th of 1942. My sister and several friends had decided to give me a surprise birthday party with fireworks, balloons, cake, homemade churned ice cream—a good ole fashioned celebration. My sister knew how depressed I had been; since the death of Bernise I had just not been the same.

Enoch knew about the surprise and had agreed to keep me "busy" while my sister and friends were outside decorating for the party. He and I were in the bedroom with little Irene. My uncle Andrew had built a cradle for her; I could touch a pedal on the cradle with my foot and it would rock until I touched the pedal again to stop it. I had just started the cradle in motion when I heard a lot of noise outside. I turned to Enoch and asked, "Do you hear that noise?" "No, I don't hear anything", he said. I thought it was the Japanese surrounding the house. I repeated, "Enoch, you had better go and see. Why, it could be the Japanese!" It was all he could do not to laugh; he did not budge. I got up and walked ever so quietly to the door. When I opened it I saw my sister and the others; they had surrounded the house. Fire works lit up the night sky. When I heard the men shoot fireworks I screamed, "Run! The Japanese are coming, run and hide!" They all yelled "Surprise, Happy Birthday!" My older sister grabbed and kissed me on the cheek. "You silly goose; it's just my Enoch and the others shooting fireworks because it's your birthday!" One of the women fell out laughing; I wanted to hit her I was so mad. When I realized that it was a celebration for me I cried tears of joy because they had gone to all of that trouble to show so much love and affection.

The next three years were full of prosperity for our growing family. My heart softened towards Enoch; after Irene, we had another girl who was born on the 14th of February 1943, which Enoch also named—Katherine. He pronounced it "Ka-tha-rene", again in my honor. Katherine was rambunctious and fun loving like her brother Lee Mark. Grace assumed the role of big sister to both Irene and Katherine; she particularly nurtured Katherine as she grew in age. In 1945 America dropped the atomic bomb on Hiroshima and Nagasaki. The United States emerged as a super power in the world and the war was over. In September of that year I had a precious little boy, whom I named after the man who had stood by me during the worst of times, Enoch. Little Enoch had beautiful brown skin, light eyes, and curly hair. He was the apple of my eye and it had been almost three years since there had been a baby in the house. Everybody loved "Skeeter".

Enoch had a baby goat that Skeeter called his very own. As a baby the goat was cute and cuddly; Skeeter played with him all the time. However, the animal grew larger and taller much faster than little Enoch. The goat was full grown with horns in no time at all; by the time Skeeter was 3 or 4 the animal had gotten so large that he was afraid of it. Everyday Skeeter would come running through the screen door on the front porch just minutes after he had gone out to play. I knew that the goat was near; the goat that Skeeter had played with since birth ran after him. "Mama, Mama", little Skeeter yelled. I would shoo the animal so that Skeeter could get up on the porch and back into the house safely. One evening when Enoch came home after working all day I decided to tell him about little Enoch and the goat. Enoch was afraid that the goat would charge the child; although we knew that the animal would never intentionally harm the boy, we both recognized that the dumb animal's weight and force could easily kill our son. Enoch was determined that he would not lose another child on that land; when darkness fell he took his shotgun out back and killed the goat.

The next day little Enoch could smell the cured wild animal as his Father barbecued its meat on an open pit. At mealtime our son, who was wise for his age, asked about his goat. Chuck said sheepishly, "You're eatin' it!" Charles, J.E., and Lee Mark laughed as Skeeter quickly spit the meat from his mouth and began to cry. He did not stop crying, "Pa killed my goat; pa killed my goat." I grabbed him and rocked him to sleep that night. Skeeter had nightmares for several weeks after the goat was killed. The dreams always ended with the goat charging after him as he tried to no avail to reach the house. He would always wake up safe and sound in his Mother's arms, just before the goat reached him.

In October of 1948 our next little boy was born; I named this boy Bennie after my uncle Bennie Coglin. Of course his Dad gave him *Franklin* as his middle name; and his older brother Lee Mark insisted on naming him Leon. Bennie

Franklin Leon Ward had such a distinguished name—one that stood out from all the rest. We did not know it at the time but he would be recognized more than all of my children for his accomplishments; the name fit! Bennie was a very large baby, weighing over 9 pounds at birth. He would not cry; he would just sit there. And little Enoch adored him; if someone looked at him or tried to hold him he would tug on my skirt and begin crying "Mama, you better get your baby; you better get your baby, Mama", as if to warn me before anyone had the chance to touch him. I thought Bennie was so stubborn. He would just sit there. It did not matter what you did he would not laugh, he would not cry, he just sat there! Over the years as I reflected on this baby, I realized that the word *pensive* provided a more appropriate description of his behavior; he was quietly observing and taking in everything. At five years old, Katherine would pick him up to assist me with him. She nicknamed him "*Bud*". Little did Katherine know how appropriate the name was; while both her younger brothers were smart, this little brother was really a *budding* genius!

In the next four years I would have two more girls: Daisy Joann in January of 1950 and Peggie, the baby girl, in September of 1952. My Mother, Ina, named the first child Daisy; I did not particularly care for the first name so I gave her *Joann* as a middle name. I called her Joann because the name fit. My baby girl was coal black at birth like Mammy. Aunt Peggie, the midwife who attended during the birth of this child, had been there through most of my childbirths. She was also a very dark attractive woman to whom I was eternally grateful; since there were no hospitals I could not have lived through all eleven births without her help. Our baby girl Peggie was named to honor this woman. As the months and years passed Peggie's complexion changed and became lighter; although she no longer had the woman's skin color, the name fit! My oldest boy, J.E., would be the first child to hold my baby girl; it was as if at that moment a special bond existed between the two of them. That bond would last his lifetime; they always seemed to have a special place in each other's hearts and lives.

The family was complete. Enoch was 45 and I was 40 years old. The oldest boy James was now 20; Charles was 19. As the boys grew older James would use every tactic possible to off-load the majority of the work to his two younger brothers, Charles and Lee Mark. They were hard working boys who knew that their Father needed their assistance with the crops and the animals to maintain the farm. By this time Enoch had built a huge home with a room for each child and two porches, front and back. The house also had a large living room, a den, a kitchen, a dining area, and a parlor so that Grace could sit in privacy with boys who came to court her. I ordered appliances, furniture, and clothes and shoes for the children C.O.D. from Sears & Roebuck, which Enoch paid for in cash upon receipt. Enoch took care of everything else; I would make a list and send him to the store for food. He bought my dresses, shoes, underwear, and even stockings. We had cars—one for Enoch and one for the boys—and any other thing that Enoch thought we wanted or needed. My Dad, James Clark, was proud to admit that he had been wrong about his son-in-law. He had been a wonderful husband to me and a great Father and provider for our children. My Dad could not have been happier with how much we had accumulated.

It was a Saturday night; we had just come in from harvesting the crops in the fields. Charles came into my bedroom and said, "Mama, I want to talk to you". "What is it, son?", I asked. I knew that something must be terribly wrong. Charles was such a kind and humble person. He must be very perturbed if he had to talk to me in private. "Mama I don't want to be a farmer. I heard some of the men talking in town about a new plant where they make bricks in Augusta. It's hard work but the pay is good. I want to go up to Augusta and try to get a job at that plant; it will be much better than giving half of what we earn from crops to our landlord. When

I get settled I'll send for the rest of you," he said. His words reminded me so much of those spoken by my Dad many years ago when I was a child. "Where will you stay?", I asked. "Aunt Louise (Enoch's younger sister) has a house not too far from the plant; she said she would let me stay there if I pay her a little each week", he replied. Deep down in my heart I always knew that the children would someday outgrow the rural area where we lived. They had so much of my Dad's spirit of independence; he was always trying to do more, to learn more, and to live more. I also knew that Enoch depended so much on Charles that he would be furious! But I could look in my son's eyes and tell that he was ready to leave, with or without my blessing. I thought it was so nice that he was respectful enough to tell us instead of just leaving. And so I hugged him and told him to just go; I would explain everything to Enoch and somehow make things right.

The next day Charles left for Augusta; at the end of the day Enoch asked about his son. Enoch was upset when I explained that Charles had moved to Augusta. "How will we make it without his help?", he asked. He was worried that he would have to pay someone to help him plow the fields. I interjected, "It won't be long. When he gets settled he's coming back to move us up there in a house, too!" "Oh no! You can go with him; I'll never follow that boy to Augusta and give up everything I've worked for all my life. My house, my own food source, everything! Have you lost your mind?", he yelled, storming out of the door.

"Well," I prayed, "Lord what must I do?" Several months passed and Lee Mark and James plowed the fields, helped pick the crops, and tended to the animals. Charles had established himself on a job at the old Babcock and Wilcox brick manufacturing plant site on Highway 56 in Augusta. He stayed in a room in his Aunt Louise's house for about a year; he paid her a small amount of rent. One week he would keep a paycheck; the next week he would send one to me to help out with things. On his days off he looked for housing.

Hornsby Subdivision was a new black neighborhood that was being built down past the County Fairgrounds. The houses were being sold by the Pilgrim Health & Life, a black owned company; the area was like a marsh. Nevertheless, the houses were very small but well built and had running water, inside toilets, electricity, and gas heat. Charles came home that year in November to move the family to Hornsby Subdivision.

Now Augusta had far more opportunities than rural Jenkins County or even the town of Millen. By comparison it was a very large city with a downtown, lots of industry, its own water source (the Savannah River), and good schools for blacks. Lucy Craft Laney High School allowed black children to complete the 12th grade. Blacks could attend a local college, Paine College, to obtain a college degree. And there was Greene's Diner and other local stores and restaurants where all of the Ward children (*that were of age*) could find part-time work. Reid's Enterprises was a new development in an area just beyond the subdivision that was owned by Charlie Reid, Sr., a local black businessman. When Charles explained to me how important it was for the children's sake to allow them to advance and be more than farmers, I quickly agreed to move. It was my task to convince Enoch that it was the right thing to do.

"How can I convince my husband to do this thing when I'm not sure myself that it is the right thing to do?" I prayed. It was as if a voice from heaven spoke to me. I just simply told him with a conviction he had not seen in me since I lost Bernise, "Enoch, I am going to take these kids and follow Charles to Augusta with or without you. If you stay here you'll stay here alone!" I was a betting woman. I bet that this man who had been with me for 22 years could not bear to live without his family and me. I was right; in September of 1953 the Ward family moved to Augusta in the house on the corner of Cherry Avenue and Rachael Street.

No one saw me because I would wait until everyone was fast asleep; then I cried all night every night. The house was so small compared to the house that I left back home. There was no way to heat the home except for gas, which was stored out back in a large tank. There was no way to know the tank was empty except that there was no heat. And we had to wait for days before a truck came to fill it again. There were thousands of big mosquitoes—I had never seen so many mosquitoes that big! My babies, Joann and Peggie, would cry at night and beg me to please take them home. Behind my house there was nothing but brush and what appeared to be desolation.

We drove the 50 miles back to Rockyford every fourth Sunday to attend the one church service held per month back home. Although there were churches in Augusta, there was not one nearby—to our knowledge. A few of us in the neighborhood would set up a tent behind my house on Sunday mornings to have Sunday school for the children. And my Dad, who would come to see me as often as he could, said that he used to run cattle through the area on horseback; he chided me that the area was once nothing but swamp land—the city's garbage dump. But through all my disillusionment I never displayed any negative feelings outwardly. To Enoch and the children I was a content woman who was completely satisfied with our new surroundings. I had prayed and asked God to make all things right in His own time; and in time He answered my prayers.

Within a few months the construction workers were building new homes behind us. The homes were occupied as fast as they were built. As each new family moved in it seemed that the mosquitoes and bugs seemed to dissipate. The gas tanks were replaced by gas lines, which were far more reliable. Stores cropped up all around. An elementary school was built within walking distance from the house. Enoch was working for Charlie Reid, Sr., who had expanded his business adjacent to the Hornsby Subdivision to include a hotel, apartments, a restaurant, a nightclub, and a bowling alley for blacks. James and Charles were both working at the brick plant; Grace, Lee Mark, and Irene finished high school in Augusta; then Grace started her first year at Paine College. Katherine, Enoch, Jr., and Bennie began attending Peter H. Craig Elementary School. I worked with Peggie and Joann at home, teaching them the basic skills—their alphabet, how to read, write, and how to add. We were crowded into the little house on the corner of Rachael Street and Cherry Avenue but somehow we managed to be happy. For the first time in our lives we had an opportunity to own our land and our home; we had our faith in God, our love for each other, and hope that every tomorrow would be better than today.

Growing Pains

The Ward children, like James Clark in his younger days, never seemed to be satisfied; they suffered from continual growing pains. The older children especially saw the vast difference in life style, culture, and opportunity that moving to Augusta had afforded them, which challenged their intellect. The rhetorical questions, "What else can I do?" and "What more can I be?" were prevalent in their minds. Their very souls ached to continually see and experience all that was possible; and so they did. Lee Mark went off to Atlantic City, New Jersey with Charles and some of his friends to work for the summer. Next Grace followed them and worked on the Boardwalk in Atlantic City during the summer; she came back home to finish Paine College. Charles grew tired of the repetitive work available in Augusta; he enlisted in the US Army during the Korean War. Lee Mark and Charles were very close; when his older brother left home, Lee Mark followed suit and went out to California. Lee Mark was drafted in the Army and served for one year. After 3 years in the Service Charles went on to California to join Lee Mark. Irene befriended a girl in high school who told her about an advertisement in the paper that read "Girls for hire". The two girls would clean up the homes of wealthy whites in New York and New Jersey in exchange for free room and board. These two girls went off to the North East as live-ins for the summer and never returned. Enoch was miserable; from his viewpoint the Ward family was falling apart.

But all things work together for good for those who love the Lord. And as only He would fix it the children who left worked and contributed to the household allowing those who remained to have physical and intellectual room to grow. While Charles was in the Army he kept half his money and sent the other half to me every month. He also sent me a $25 US Savings bond; he continued sending the bonds after he began working in California, all of which I kept in a safe at home until the late 1980's. My Dad taught me to save so I always kept money for a rainy day; but no one ever imagined that I had never cashed in a single one of the bonds during all of those months and years. When I returned some of the bonds to Charles, almost 30 years later, he could not believe their value! The older bonds had not only matured but had earned interest and were worth far more than he had originally invested.

James remained at home until he married Thelma. During the years that he stayed at home he purchased a car that Grace drove to college and to work. He also gave his Dad and me rent money, which I used to pay for Grace's college tuition. Grace finished Paine College and began teaching English at John S. Davidson Junior High School. She stayed at home, did the first renovations to the house, and helped to make sure that the last four children had every thing that they needed and then some! In addition, she paid us rent. Now their Father had always been frugal so instead of being able to save half of what he earned he had begun to save almost all of what he earned. We never forgot how much our children helped us; as the children grew older and needed financial assistance, they had only to ask and we gave back to them freely.

When Grace began teaching, Bennie attended her school. She would come home every day and tell me how very smart he was. "He makes 100 on everything we give him, Mom", she'd say. All of my children were extremely smart; but from the time Bennie was 3 or 4 years old, I knew he was beyond being just smart—I knew that he had a special level of intelligence. My children were always proud of the accomplishments of their siblings. The older ones took particular pride in the accomplishments of the younger ones, because they realized that they shared in their upbringing.

First, let me just say that I have always felt as if I brought up two sets of children—the first 6 and the last 4. There was such a disparity in ages between these two groups and I matured so much during the first 15 years of my marriage, until by the time these four youngsters were interacting with me and each other, so much had changed; I know that I changed my approach in many ways. And yet in many respects the more things changed the more they stayed the same. I still trained them up in the admonition of the Lord; I taught them to be careful and take care of everything. And as always, I taught the last four to love and look out for each other—just as I did with the older ones.

There were many childhood experiences that these four children shared. I'll recount two of my most memorable ones. The first was a lesson in survival. Joann and Peggie always loved Enoch, Jr. and Bennie. If the boys were not picking on them these two little girls were aggravating the boys. Enoch, Jr. and Bennie had gone over to Reid's Enterprises to the hotel. Skeeter and his friend Tom used to work part time for Enoch picking up paper around the pool; since Enoch, Jr. had ready access to the pool he learned to swim like a fish. He and Charlie, Jr., the owner's son, were also very good friends. The boys would hang around the pool, sometimes for hours. Bennie often tagged along with his older brother. Now as it would naturally just fall into place Joann idolized her big brother Enoch and Peggie just adored her big brother Bennie. No matter what the two brothers did it was just fine with these two little sisters, as long as they could hang around. One day Joann and Peggie asked me if they could go for a picnic; they were going to sit under the tree and watch their brothers (from a distance) as they swam in the pool. I made them teacakes and gave them a couple of sandwiches with two Coca Cola's in a little basket, a little blanket for them to sit on, and of course they took their paper dolls.

Since Enoch worked at the place my kids could freely use the pool, eat at the restaurant, and play games at the bowling alley. Well they could hardly get out of the door that the little girls across and down the street were not following them. The girls decided after they had eaten and played with the paper dolls for a while that they would pester their brothers. Anyway Nelson, the older Reid boy, appeared and Joann and one of the other little girls had a crush on him. They decided to get closer to the pool; however, the girls did not know how to swim and were afraid of the water. They were also afraid that their brothers might drown, so they began saying, "You better get out of that water; you're going to drown". The boys had repeatedly told them to go back under the tree and play; they wanted to be left alone. But these little girls were determined to get as close to the boys and what they were doing as possible. So the boys decided that they would have a little fun and throw Joann and Peggie in the pool.

Now Joann was the oldest but Peggie had the longest legs. Peggie managed to run away; before Joann could move Enoch, Jr. had grabbed her and thrown her into the deep end of the pool. She could not swim but her Clark spirit for survival had her kicking and moving her feet; she imitated the movements she had seen her favorite brother make and finally made it over to the side of the pool. In the meantime Peggie (thinking that Joann was going to drown) had sprinted back to the house and was standing in the door; she told the entire story and had me headed out the door running to *save* my child. Of course by the time I got there Joann was playing in the water as if nothing had happened. "Mama, I can swim!" she exclaimed. Enoch, Jr., Bennie, Tom, and little Charlie were just laughing. Although I did not spank Skeeter I did chastise him for his reckless behavior. Of course in my heart I knew he had inadvertently done a very good thing—he had helped his little sister overcome her fear of water. As a result she can swim like a fish, too!

The second incident proved to be educational for the entire family; we all learned that we had a genius in our midst! For weeks Bennie had sat around reading Webster's dictionary. He had inherited my photographic memory; if he saw something his brain remembered it. Once he figured this out he used it to his advantage—on tests at school, at home, everywhere and in every way possible. Now each child was given an allowance every week. Joann and Peggie really did not have to spend their money on anything; plus Peggie got a dollar a week from J.E. and an occasional dollar from Billy, who would also send her trunk loads of clothes, shoes, and toys. Bennie never liked physical labor; in fact I teased him many times about being lazy. He would look at me and say, "Mama, when I grow up I am going to use my brain not my muscles to make a living; you'll see."

His first successful enterprise was established right here at home. He would charge the girls a fee to design and build cars for their paper dolls; they also had to be able to tell him who was depicted on a randomly selected baseball card before he would do the work. And when Peggie and the little girl next door got Barbie Doll Houses for Christmas, he assembled Peggie's dollhouse to perfection free of charge. The neighbor's child paid him a nice little fee for his expertise. He then began to challenge his little sisters to turn to any page in the dictionary and choose any word; he told them that he could recite the definition verbatim. If he recited the definition correctly they would have to get him a cold soda or a snack from the kitchen; if he missed one, well, tough luck for them! Of course he had memorized the entire Webster's dictionary ensuring that he would never lose this little game. His sisters, even at that age, could not imagine that anyone let alone their big brother could accomplish such a feat. So they challenged him over and over again; Peggie would come to me complaining and I would admonish them all about playing such a game. And yet they participated anyway. The girls began to notice that they were constantly *serving* Bennie; they finally figured out that they could not win! They enjoyed the idea of challenging their big brother and I realized that via this game the girls were learning—they were expanding their vocabulary! I also recognized that the Lord had given Bennie a very special gift. However, it was only after Bennie took an IQ test at school that it finally sank in: *my baby boy was a genius!*

The children were all competitive, a trait which carried over into their academic experiences. On-lookers who saw how well my children excelled probably thought that they were taught to compete with the other students at school. Wrong! My children were competing with each other because of pressure! That's right—not peer pressure but sibling pressure! Since the older siblings had such high standards of achievement each of the younger children was motivated by an older sibling to accomplish even more than the others. And because each child was always trying to do as well or better than his or her siblings Enoch and I did not have to ask about homework, or to make sure that tasks were achieved correctly, or to push them; they studied and completed their assignments on their own. Eventually *sibling motivation* became *self-motivation.*

Before we moved to Augusta Enoch and Katherine had been allowed to skip a grade in school; little Enoch was 16 when he graduated from Lucy C. Laney high school as its valedictorian. Bennie, Joann, and Peggie all started school when they were 5 years old; they were slightly younger than some of their classmates, graduating at the age of 17. Bennie had the highest average in his class; Joann and Peggie had very high averages, too. These children went to school in historical times. My children saw television go from black and white to color. They experienced slide rules, calculators, and computers. They rode buses, trains, and flew on airplanes. They saw telephones go from party lines to private lines. And they all had cars of their own; most of them learned how to drive. They saw men orbit the Earth and walk on the moon. They lived by the principles that we had taught them—James Clark's principles for success, most of which were biblically based.

My children saw our nation at its worse and its best. I gave them the foundation that my parents gave me. We made sure that every one of them was baptized; and as long as they lived under our roof they attended Church with their Father and me. We bought them all that they needed; with the help of my older children the younger ones never went without food, clothing, or any other thing that children from smaller more affluent families had. And yet they all faced racism and violence—especially while they were in school. They reaped the benefits of the struggles of folks like Martin Luther King. Jr., they watched his famous March on Washington, D.C. and then heard the news about his assassination. They were in school when it was announced that John F. Kennedy, Jr. was assassinated and they watched and waited as students rioted at major universities across the nation. As impressionable young adults they saw television broadcasts of the War in Vietnam and experienced firsthand the *hippie* movement. They heard the resounding voices of the black militants and liberal radicals; they studied all of the different African American and pan African theologies with all the philosophies on racism and hatred that flourished in the nation. Enoch and I sat there with them, watching and listening to their doubts and their fears, and encouraging them and supporting them every step of the way. They chose to believe in Christianity; through it all we trusted in God and He delivered us.

Now while these children were encountering their issues with race and discrimination I was going through my own set of personal issues. I was struggling with obesity. Some people eat because they are miserable, some eat because they are happy, and some eat because they are bored. I ate because I loved to cook and eat! My husband managed a grocery store and would buy any kind of food the children and I wanted. I would read magazines and cookbooks to get ideas for new dishes; I would cook samples and taste them (sometimes eat the whole thing). Once I got the dish perfected I would prepare it for our meal and eat some more; this cycle usually occurred in the same day!

You probably recall that in a previous chapter and paragraph I wrote about how as a young woman I was "*tailor made*". Well, let me tell you after 10 children and cooking and tasting all those different meals the tailor practically had to make my dresses! I was well over 200 pounds by the time these younger children were teens. My husband would look at me adoringly but I would see him flirt and smile at women who still had their young girlish figures. I would sing, pray, and ask God to take away my feelings of self-consciousness—these were foreign and distressful to me because I had always been very secure and confident about my appearance.

God rarely answers prayers the way we expect but He does answer them in the right way and at the right time. I woke up one morning covered in welts; my face was red with blisters. Grace was still at home so she immediately took me to my family physician, Dr. Brown, who sent me to a specialist. The new doctor quickly determined that I had an allergic reaction to some food types. He prescribed Benadryl for the allergy and suggested a change in diet. I was so sick of my bloated unattractive countenance that I decided right then and there that I would hold myself responsible for my appearance (my weight) in the same way I had accepted responsibility for every other aspect of my life. I made a change in my eating habits—not so much in what I ate but how I prepared it and how much I ate! The doctor monitored my weight loss and watched as I went down from over 200 pounds to about 145 pounds. I began to watch exercise shows on television and to run in place, touch my toes, and do floor exercises on a daily basis. With the exercise and weight loss came lower blood pressure and the return of an elevated level of self-confidence.

My girls, especially Joann, would buy me gorgeous dresses, suits, blouses, and ensembles made by the better clothiers to encourage my continued effort. I accumulated the most beautiful expensive outfits in sizes 14 and 16 instead of size 22! And because I changed my exercise and eating habits gradually I saw a continual change in my weight and general health that I have been able to maintain to this day. Now that I'm in a Nursing Home, I still watch what and how much I eat. And guess what? People are still telling me "You're Beautiful!" Today people love to blame other things and other people for every thing that happens to them instead of accepting ownership of their circumstances and taking control of the situation—handling their own issues. Yes, my family and I have had our set of trials and tribulations—still do! But we pray and ask God for guidance. We live by one of my Dad's old principles—"You take one step and He'll take two"—an expression that has encouraged us all through the most desperate of times to keep the Faith. We never stop trying . . . . *If at first you don't succeed, try, try again*—that's my motto!

Upward Bound

When the younger four children, Enoch, Jr., Bennie, Joann, and Peggie, were small I took them with me to the downtown stores. There would be signs posted over restroom doors and water fountains that said "Coloreds" or "Whites Only". If you ask my younger ones if they remember these signs they will probably tell you "NO". I always tried to shelter them from personally experiencing racism. I told them about racial divides that existed between blacks and whites; at the same time I taught them that in God's sight they were equal to any person, regardless of color. We always discussed current events; I subscribed to the newspaper and Enoch and I made sure we had a black and white floor model television as soon as we got settled in our home. And of course we had the old party-line telephone—an essential for staying in touch with Lee Mark, Charles, and Irene.

Now when I say that I sheltered them I do not mean that I would not allow them to experience things on their own; in fact when Bennie was still very young I would send him on errands alone on the bus at times. All the children were academically and socially inclined. I taught them, as my parents before me, to work hard then play hard. They all tried to have little jobs primarily for extra spending money. The older children did housekeeping or were waiters at tables. When Katherine was a teenager she was so loved by the woman she worked for that the family took her to the beach with them on family vacations. There were not many little black children who had been to Myrtle Beach or Hilton Head for summer vacation; and she came back having been treated very well and all the more learned from the experience.

Enoch had a brother and sister who lived in St. Augustine, Florida and I had two brothers and a sister in Savannah. We took a family vacation almost every summer while the children were out of school; we went to St. Augustine or Savannah, sometimes both places. The children loved to visit the Alligator Farm and the Fountain of Youth in St. Augustine. And the beach at Savannah was also a favorite; Enoch and the boys would go crabbing and the children would feast on their bounty!

Little Enoch started with a newspaper route; and although I would shake my head and ask "Why?" (It was such a mess and so much trouble for so little money), I sat back and waited until he realized on his own that it was "much ado about nothing". For his next job he caddied at the Augusta National; he was really too small to caddy but he would go anyway. He learned how to play golf as a caddy at the Augusta National and to this day his favorite pastime is a round of golf. Bennie was a pitcher for the school's baseball team. Joann and Peggie played the flute and clarinet, respectively, in the school's band. Peggie also sang in a trio for one of her elementary school teachers, Mr. Jerry Harris (who was also a pianist); he would carry her with the other girls to perform concerts at various civic functions. As a treat after their performance, he would take them all out to eat in a nice restaurant. I encouraged them all to have extra-curricular activities to balance their study time. They were very smart so they never spent too much time studying and as I said before they all wanted to make good grades. They were never *paid* for good grades; instead we encouraged them to do their best at everything and to finish what they started. Their inherent desire to be the best that they could be at whatever the task was coupled with determination; the result—they were successful!

At 16 Enoch, Jr. received a full scholarship to Paine College. He enjoyed being at Paine College, like his sisters Katherine and Grace, before him. After his second year Mr. Webster, a white man, approached him about transferring to the Georgia Institute of Technology, in Atlanta, Georgia. He told him that he would extend a personal student loan for tuition that could be repaid after graduation. There were just two *small* issues. Always keep in mind that the size of an issue depends on your point of view! First Enoch, Jr. was underage—so he could not sign any legally binding note. This issue was quickly resolved when he asked Grace, who was now teaching school, to co-sign the note. Grace agreed of course. The second tiny issue related to housing. Our *Skeeter* would have to stay in the dormitory in Atlanta, Georgia. No big deal, right? Wrong! He would be the first black student ever to be allowed to live in the dormitory. Well Enoch Ward, Sr. was adamant that his child—his namesake—would not be killed in Atlanta—just for the sake of integration! Enoch, Jr. wanted to go; it was an opportunity of a lifetime and so he went. As with the others, I allowed him to go on up there and I smoothed it over with his Dad.

He attended the school almost without incident; he was fairly small in stature but very handsome with light eyes like mine. And he got along with most of the boys and girls that he met at the school. He probably went through several roommates before someone would stay in the room with him but he never complained. Of all of my children's temperaments his was the most predictable—at least I thought so until the day he picked a student up and threw him straight out of the window in anger! Now I knew he had to be provoked in order for him to react so violently. I was right. The students had been making racial slurs at him for some time; he had ignored the slurs (as we had told him) and always reminded himself that he was there to get the best education possible—nothing more, nothing less. But this night the boys on the floor where he lived had planned to see just how far they could push him. One of the boys waited until Enoch, Jr. was in their midst to talk about his experiences working part-time as a police officer on the weekend. The boy told about patrolling the West End area, a predominantly black area where Morehouse, Clark, Spellman, and Morris Brown colleges were located. This young man laughed about beating black college boys who were caught walking at night for no reason.

Enoch, Jr. was disgusted and walked away. As he walked swiftly away one of the boys grabbed his shoulder; Skeeter did not look back to see who it was and in his mind he thought that the boy who had boasted about this behavior towards blacks had decided to attack him. Enoch, Jr. would later say that before he knew it he was yelling "Get your hands off me, don't touch me!", and had picked the boy up and thrown him out of the window. Skeeter was hurt when he realized it was a friend, a white boy who was really trying to console and encourage him. Needless to say Skeeter met with the Dean who smiled and said that he was surprised that he had gone that long without an incident. The friend did not press charges and Enoch, Jr. went on to become the first black Chemical Engineer to graduate from Georgia Tech. It was an important accomplishment for Enoch, Jr., the school, and the other black students; Enoch, Jr. proved that it was possible for a black person to obtain a Chemical Engineering degree from Georgia Tech. But equally important was the effect that his success had on his younger brother and sisters. They were led by his example to pursue the best education possible irrespective of the location or racial make-up of the school they chose to attend. And it gave his Father courage, too. He was able to put aside his fears for them and let them go on to achieve their goals and realize their dreams. Enoch, Jr. was a Chemical Engineer for Dow Chemical, Corning, and Proctor and Gamble. He was a vice president for Proctor and Gamble just prior to retiring to become a realtor and contractor. He is now the pastor of First Metropolitan Baptist Church here in Augusta.

Grace was involved in a program called Upward Bound at Paine College. Upward Bound was a government-funded program targeted at helping poor black kids (today they are referred to as "at-risk") become prepared for college. To qualify a child had to show the potential for being a college student but have low-income levels and other risk factors (single parent, live in the projects, work to help family, etc.) that might prevent them from attempting college. Although my children did not qualify (imagine that—they did not qualify for something!) Joann was allowed to participate because Grace was a teacher and counselor in the program. There were classes and activities for the students on the weekends and each student was given a small stipend for participating. One summer Joann represented Paine's group by attending a summer camp at Yale University in New Haven, Connecticut. We allowed her to participate so that she would get a feel for being away from home in case she wanted to go off to college. I could write a book about all the things Joann taught me when she returned. Let me tell you I look back on it and admire myself for my open-mindedness; we'll save that for another book. If your children have an opportunity to participate in summer programs and camps, let them go. It helps them to adjust better when they go off to college. Bennie participated in the Governor's Honors program and Peggie was a participant in the National Science Foundation's summer camp.

Ever since my children first started school in Augusta, I was always being told by teachers and principals alike that they were not only smart but also well disciplined and well mannered. So it was no surprise when the School Board decided to implement a Freedom of Choice policy, which equated to de-segregation for the schools in Augusta, the teachers came and asked if I would allow Bennie, Joann, and Peggie to participate in the process. Enoch and I discussed it with Grace. We trusted Grace's input since she was a part of the school system and knew all the details. We had just let our son, Enoch, Jr., go off to Georgia Tech in Atlanta. Grace had really helped convince her Dad that what Skeeter was doing was good and right. She also reminded us that the white schools had better books, better facilities, the best teachers, and that the children would have a chance to earn scholarships to schools away from Augusta, schools other than Paine College.

Now don't get me wrong, Paine College was and still is a good black school. Grace went there and became known as one of the best English teachers in Augusta. And Katherine, who worked with the lower grades, was also very good and well trained. Not to mention that it was because of the Upward Bound program at Paine that Joann (and I) became exposed to Yale University. But I always hoped and dreamed that my children's education would not be bound by race— only by choice. Still it was a tough decision for us because our children were destined to be "*firsts*" if they stayed at their respective schools. We would be moving them from a comfort zone to an unknown. And we were not sure if we were ready to deal with all of the different issues—things that might happen—if we allowed them to be a part of this *desegregation*. I was particularly concerned about Bennie, who would be a senior at Laney the next year. He was so smart that he was going to be the school's valedictorian. We prayed first and then asked the children if they wanted to try it. Our anxiety was countered by their excitement; we trusted God to show us all the way and pressed on towards the mark on higher ground!

At 16 Bennie started his senior year at the high school,

the Academy of Richmond County; it was a military academy so Bennie participated in ROTC. Joann would have been a sophomore at Laney; she and Peggie went to Tubman Jr. High School. Parents had to provide their children's transportation; Grace would carry them to the city bus stop where they would take the public transit to and from school. My three babies, Bennie, Joann, and Peggie, had to endure a lot to go to white schools back then. Although it was difficult it paid off for them in the end.

The few blacks in Bennie's class got the brunt of the hatred; they were the first group to break the barrier. Eggs were thrown, teachers discriminated—you name it and they encountered it. Bennie made A's on everything he was given; no matter how difficult my little genius aced it! He had the highest average in the school; but because he had not attended the school more than one year he was denied the right to be the class valedictorian. I felt so bad for him because I knew that it was not fair. I felt that the white parents just did not want a black student to be valedictorian! If that was not bad enough, Bennie's Chemistry class took a trip to Oak Ridge National Laboratories in Oakridge, Tennessee during the school year. The white woman teacher informed us that Bennie could go if we were willing to pay the extra rate for a full room. Since none of the parents would allow their boys to share a room with a black boy my son had to stay in a room alone; the other kids shared rooms and only had to pay half the room rate. Now I considered this tactic as a subtle method of denying him the right to participate; I always wondered if they thought that we would not be able to afford to send him. Grace and I asked him if he still wanted to go; he said yes and so we paid the extra rate. I look back on that time at how far God has brought him; he has been truly blessed!

At the age of 17 Bennie, who scored a near perfect score on the SAT and college placement tests, won a full four-year scholarship to the Massachusetts Institute of Technology in Cambridge, Massachusetts where he earned double degrees in Mathematics and in Physics. Bennie went on to Princeton University in Princeton, New Jersey where he received his Masters and Ph.D. degrees in High-Energy Physics. He has worked at the Stanford Linear Accelerator Center, CERN in Switzerland, and has had an appointment to the MAXPLANK Institute in Germany. He has taught physics at Princeton, Purdue, Stanford, and the University of Tennessee at Knoxville. He is now an internationally known high-energy physicist who has given speeches all over the United States and the world about his theories on the Standard Model, whatever that is! I often wonder if his trip to Oakridge sparked his interest in Physics; if so then the full room rate was worth it!

Now Joann came home with very few incidents to report. She was always level headed and well grounded; she handled everything. She attended the school's classes and activities and was friendly with the other students. Although she worked after school she was in the Senior Choir, the Beta Club, and other activities and still made excellent grades. When Enoch, Jr. finished college he bought a new Camaro and gave Joann his little white Chevrolet Corvair. It was his little car and he wanted her to have it. Now you know I had this thing about all my girls learning to drive. So when Grace was old enough, J.E. taught her to drive; Grace taught Katherine, Enoch, Bennie, Joann, and Peggie. (I know, I left out Irene—Grace tried with her, but it didn't work out!)

Well Joann had been driving her little car around the neighborhood. My rule was that if they could back the car out of the driveway without going into the ditch on either side, they could drive. Anyway it was time for Joann to get her license and Grace had gone somewhere to a workshop; Joann was determined to get her license. She asked me if she could take the Corvair for a drive; her Dad was gone so I said yes. She drove her car to the driver's license bureau downtown, got out, went in and took the test. When the officer asked her, "Who brought you down here?", she said "My Mom brought me; she's across the street shopping in the basement at White's". She passed the written test; the Officer took her on the short road test and gave her the license. Of course she drove herself home!

When she came home and told me this story (my kids would always tell me everything) I was astonished that she had told a lie to get her way. I did not punish her with a spanking but I punished her with words. I know that she felt bad about what she had done. However, my children knew that once an issue was addressed it was a done deal—sea of forgetfulness—where I was concerned. I did not teach any of them to harbor bad feelings because of a bad deed. Anyway, from that day forward Dad would go to work and Joann and Peggie would go to school in the little white Corvair. Because of her good grades she received a full scholarship to Mercer University in Macon, Georgia. I never will forget the Sunday we took her down to school; Grace drove above the speed limit all the way to Macon. When an Officer pulled her over I asked him why he wasn't in Church. Grace still got the speeding ticket but it made me feel better! Joann drove her little Corvair back and forth to school after the first year. She went on to become an Engineering Manager for Rockwell's Space Shuttle program in Downey, California and is now employed in Engineering at Boeing.

Peggie on the other hand had both good and bad experiences. When she was at Tubman, Mrs. Adams, a white math teacher, recognized that she was smart. Mrs. Adams asked Peggie if she were transferred to Richmond would she be willing to take Algebra II and Geometry at the same time so that she could take Calculus her senior year. Joann was going to Richmond the next year so she jumped at the chance. I didn't know it then but this one decision made a tremendous difference in my baby's education. First and foremost it was proof that the black school she attended was not as advanced as the white schools. She had been in all the best classes in her old school and yet she was not advanced. She went to Richmond and made A's in both the math courses and many others; from then on she was placed in advanced classes at Richmond.

Because of this decision Peggie took Senior Math as a junior. She made all A's; B's in gym. When she got to the Senior Math Class the teacher would take off 5 points on her paper for something that would result in a single point deduction on the papers of her white peers. She would come home upset, with a feeling of helplessness. She talked to the man but her discussions were useless. Of course it made the teacher angry that she was bold (like me) enough to take the papers up to him and question his actions. Finally, Bennie called from MIT; she asked to speak to him. She told him what was happening and that she was afraid she would not get the A she deserved in the class because of this man's grading policy. He gave her the best advice a big brother could give his little sister; he encouraged her and told her that she should just study as hard as she could for the exam. Since the final exam counted the most, if she made 100, she could still receive an A. She took his advice, studied really hard, and made a 98 on the exam—the highest grade on the test in the class. One of the white girls who had befriended Peggie later told her that the teacher had made a remark that only one person in the class scored above 95; he said that if she did it they all should have been able to do it. Well, when she told me what the girl said I gasped, "I am sorry for him! He just did not know that he was dealing with one of my kids!" We both laughed. It reminded me again of my Father's old saying about adversity being an opportunity. I was proud of my little girl!

She got an A in the class, kept her A average, and spent the summer that year at the Summer Science Training Program of the National Science Foundation at Louisiana State University in Baton Rouge, Louisiana. How did she get there? Remember the teacher who took Bennie to

Oakridge? Peggie took Chemistry from that same woman, Mrs. Otwell. She noticed that Peggie excelled in Chemistry, Physics, Math, and everything else. This woman saw that Peggie was doing her best to follow in Bennie's footsteps. Only two students from Richmond were selected for the program—Peggie and a white boy.

Now if you recall in the summer of 1969 the riots were taking place in Augusta and everywhere else in the nation. Baton Rouge was known for its racism and yes, I was concerned for my baby's safety. But as God would have it Enoch, Jr. was living in Baton Rouge working as an engineer for Dow Chemical. He met Peggie at the airport and saw to it that she was settled into the school. When she got there she found that there was only one other black girl in the program—a girl from New Orleans. Her roommate who had been selected by handwriting analysis, was a redheaded freckled white girl named Debbie who was from New Boston, Texas. Although Peggie and this girl argued at first by the end of the summer Peggie and Debbie became the best of friends. With the help and constant involvement of her big brother, Enoch, Jr., both the girl and Peggie came to realize that whites and blacks could peacefully coexist and even be friends. Enoch, Jr. led this friendship by being an example to them both. He had a very good white friend in Louisiana; he and his friend (and their families) would invite Peggie and Debbie out to have dinner with them. The two families, black and white, showed these two girls how much they cared for each other. It softened both their hearts and they began to look at each other's inner selves instead of the outer skin color. In fact Debbie asked Peggie to be in her wedding.

Now I could go on and on with the stories about Peggie's summer (that'll have to be in the next book, too). But my little girl really heard and saw how white children hated blacks. Her brother led her by example to realize that people of different colors can get along and enjoy a friendship. I was so proud of Enoch, Jr. for helping her to grow in this way. She grew up in other ways, too. It was the first time that she had been away from home without me. She learned that she could survive, make decisions, and live successfully, independent of her Mom and Dad. When she returned she had cut her hair; she was still tall, lanky, and pretty (I thought all my kids were good looking) but she had matured. I knew then she would not stay here with me after high school.

She came back to Richmond at 16 and took college Calculus, Advanced Chemistry, Advanced Physics, and every advanced course available. She scored high marks on the SAT and all the placement tests; she was in the Senior Choir at school, the Beta Club, the Science Club, and in Jr. Achievement. She was a 3-time Governors Honors Program nominee and a National Merit Finalist; she had so many honors that she was Richmond's only black student to be recognized in the school's yearbook as an Outstanding Senior in 1970. She so wanted to go off to school near her big brother (Bennie) in Massachusetts and she did! She received a General Motors scholarship to Smith College in Northampton, Massachusetts where she graduated with a degree in mathematics. We did not know about the scholarship until she and I read an article about her in the Augusta Chronicle, the local newspaper. The article said that she was one of four winners of the GM scholarship in Georgia; I think she was as surprised as I was to see the announcement in the paper!

Now, I did not know it at the time but Smith College was the prestigious Ivy League girls' school that Julie Nixon Eisenhower, Nancy Reagan, and Barbara Bush had attended (among others). My little girl had really stepped out and I was so proud! When she was a junior her favorite brother Bennie, bought a brand new Porsche; he gave Peggie an early graduation present—his almost new Volkswagen Beetle. Remember that I never learned how to drive; but when he gave her the car I agreed to take the long ride with her so that she could have the car at school during her senior year.

MISTAKE! First, neither this child nor I had a clue about reading maps. She had always gone up to school with her brother; so like most young people she never worried about directions. She drove almost 2 hours in the wrong direction! I wanted to go back home but she insisted on turning around and heading North; so we did. We finally reached Baltimore, Maryland where we planned to stop and spend the night with Grace and her family. It was late and we were exhausted. We got up the next day to drive on to Northampton, Massachusetts. While we were driving across the George Washington Bridge in New York a transfer truck came reeling past us! The little car seemed to be picked up by the force of the truck almost as if we were going to be swept over the bridge and into the river below. She said, "Mom, do you feel the car lifting up, pushing over towards the rail?" "No, honey, I don't feel a thing", I would reply. She would say, "Are you sure? I thought I felt the car move." I would say, "Uh-uh, just keep driving, you're doing fine". All the time, I was praying, "Lord just get me off this bridge alive and I promise whatever I did to deserve this I won't do again". He answered my prayers and we finally made it to the *Quad* where we parked in front of Gardiner House to unload our luggage. Peggie drove her little Volkswagen Beetle her senior year. She won a GM Graduate Fellowship to Georgia Tech for the Masters degree program; she drove that little car all through her two years of graduate school. Since then she has worked in both engineering and with computers for General Motors, E. I. DuPont, Rockwell International, BNFP, Babcock & Wilcox, Graniteville, and Avondale.

We all (most of her siblings flew in to see her graduate) attended her graduation from Smith College; it was an historic moment for the college and for us. Peggie was one of 50 black graduates of Smith College that year (1974), the largest black enrollment in a class in the school's history. As for the Ward family, she was the last of the *Mohicans*, so to speak. All of my children have made me proud and as you can just imagine I never tire of bragging and boasting about their accomplishments. I look back on their journeys. Just imagine that they left home as teenagers (16 and 17 years old) who had never been away from us for any length of time; they returned home each year wiser and more independent than the year before. I cried when each one left me and I rejoiced each time they returned. I am so proud of them all. When people ask me what I did to be able to have 10 successful children I usually smile and say that I just brought them up in the admonition of the Lord, just as my parents did before me.

Higher Ed

The most important lessons that we learn in life are often not in school but through life's experiences. My children, through various stages of their growth and development, provided me with a rich and extensive higher education. Now remember that I was brought up in an environment where one critical part of the parent's role included being a good communicator, which involves being a good talker and a good listener. As I reminisce many important lessons learned come to mind.

Lesson One: There is nothing to fear but fear itself *otherwise known as you can tell your children what to do but you never know what they are really going to do so you might as well "Let go and let God".* I recall that I very seldom left the children but there was one Sunday when it was storming and I was going to Church and the boys did not want to go. A bad storm was coming our way so I told the kids that they could stay home as long as they stayed in the house. Lee Mark was a toddler; J.E. was the oldest so I left him in charge. Instead of staying in the house as I instructed J.E. and Chuck (Charles) went out onto the porch. The lightning was flashing and the thunder rolling; each time the boys heard

PEGGIE WARD KOON, PH.D.

the thunder and saw the lightning they would laugh. When I came back home I found them outside just enjoying the thunder and lightning display in the sky. I immediately told them to get into the house; I was afraid that they would be struck by one of the sharp bolts.

Now I don't know if they were laughing to hide their fear or if they just did not comprehend the severity of the weather. Although I knew it already it made me realize, as the children did, that God was in control. No matter what storms life bring we should keep laughing and smiling, for He will protect us. If God brings us to it He will bring us through it. And after the rain there was a beautiful rainbow and the sun shone so brightly; the air was fresh and the crops and flowers had been watered. What a beautiful blessing we had received!

Lesson Two: Things are seldom what they seem, especially with children *otherwise known as children know how to be manipulative too, so the rule "Believe half of what you hear and none of what you see" should be applied until further notice.* Now my husband rarely spanked any of the children; he left the discipline to me since they were not prone to misbehave. If they disobeyed me I would slap them on their leg or bottom with my hand right then; most of the time I could look at them and they would stop. If their Dad got involved it was either serious or it affected one of his favorites. You know parents rarely admit it, but sometimes they have a favorite child. I don't know why it's not discussed because it does happen. It's no different than relationships that are formed with people outside of a family; you get along with some people better than others. Call it kindred spirits, like minds—whatever the rationale—the same kinds of issues exist within a family because of personalities and preferences.

Anyway when we were still on the farm two of my girls were out in the yard playing. I could not afford to buy them real dolls so they would take old Coca Cola bottles and cut out paper models from my catalogs; they would take the paper figures and stuff them into the bottles and pretend that they were real. Well the younger of these two girls always was good with putting things together and making them look nice; she loved to decorate! My other daughter, although she had other talents, just could not make her bottle look as pretty as her sister's creation. Since she was older she decided to take her sister's "*doll*". My first inclination was to discipline the older child; instead I decided to sit back and watch to see how these two handled the situation. Well the little sister was a scrapper! She grabbed her doll back and hit her sister—hard enough to make her cry. Now I watched the entire incident waiting to see the outcome before I intervened. I thought it funny that God had given the smaller of these two the fortitude (and strength) to stand up to the older much bigger child. Before I knew it the younger child was laughing because she had managed to retrieve her property without anybody's help; the older child had run straight pass me to her Dad.

Now Enoch, because the older child was one of his favorites, had immediately run to her rescue without getting all of the details—all he knew was that the younger child had hit her sister. He got a small switch and went over to spank my little girl's legs and she ran. That little sister ran faster than a bolt of lightning and squatted in the tall grass so that her legs were completely hidden by her long flowing dress. Her Dad hit the dress 3 or 4 times with a switch missing her legs completely; she yelled as if he was really spanking her! He walked off content that he had rescued the older girl and disciplined the younger one; the younger child waited until she was sure that he was far away and then got up and ever so slowly came over to me while pretending to wipe her *dry* eyes of tears, brandishing a sheepish grin on her face. I sat back in my rocker thinking to myself about the years ahead with both of these girls. Both would prove to be challenges; time after time I saw the older child rescued by her Father. And as for the younger child, well I learned a lesson from her that day; I always knew that no matter what she encountered she would always be able to stand her ground! And if she was crying, which was rare, I always looked twice to make sure it was real!

Lesson Three: Make sure your children really understand what you mean by what you say to them *otherwise known as assume nothing, give examples to be sure your meaning is clearly understood.* For example, you want to teach your children about pride and self-worth but keep in mind that there is such a thing as teaching your children to think too much of themselves. I had always taught my children about their rich heritage; they were taught to *choose* their company. And they rarely ever heard me belittle any one; I might explain to them very delicately that they did not need to associate with certain types of children. Usually such a statement was based on moral character displayed and not on worldly possession. I would say, "We are better persons than this or that", but always referring to behavior rather than a person or station in life. Well I seldom got called to the school for any of my children's behavior but this day I received a call. The principal explained that Katherine had been in a fight on the playground.

Since my children knew that they were automatically wrong until I was convinced that the teacher was not right, I could not imagine anything other than a situation where my poor child was provoked. Still I kept an open mind. It was possible but not likely that Katherine had caused the fight. I was wrong! Katherine did not know it but as a family we were still struggling month to month and groping to find our place, both socially and economically, in the community. Enoch and I had never had a cross word with neighbors or other parents at the school. And my little girl had decided that she would chide and tease another girl about the holes in her clothes!

The girl turned around and grabbed Katherine's dress

to rip a hole in it. Remember, Katherine was rambunctious and all my girls were tom boyish because of their brothers; so when the girl tore her dress Katherine hit her—hit her hard, hard enough to make her mad and hit back. The teacher on the grounds broke up the fight and they were both disciplined at school. I did not spank Katherine again; but I did explain to her that what she did was wrong. She learned a valuable lesson and so did I! I learned that as parents we must be careful how we convey our values to our children. I wanted them to understand that people come from different backgrounds and circumstances and that what a person wears or how s/he dresses or anything physical does not define the person; a person's character—their actions, behavior, and morals—that is what really matters. I used this story with the younger children time and time again to bring home the fact: *"It's what's on the inside that really counts!"*

Lesson Four: **Always keep your lines of communication open,** *otherwise known as you might as well discuss sex with your children because they will learn it from someone else anyway.* Now keep in mind that I grew up in a time and place where sex was not discussed. I walked around in panties and bra in front of my children so that they would not be ashamed of their sexuality. I openly discussed most issues the girls brought to me; the boys discussed their sexual issues with their Dad. As old fashioned as he was Lord only knows what he told them! My older girls rarely discussed sexual topics with me when they were young; but the younger two taught me more than I wanted to know. Remember that Joann went off to Yale when she was still in high school. She met black kids from the inner cities of most of the states. She had always had a little boyfriend in school; he would sneak a kiss or put a love letter in her book bag but that was about all there was to it. So since the girls never told me about any desire that they had or any incident where a boy had approached them about having sex, I never gave it another thought.

At any rate Joann came into the kitchen where I was

busily preparing our meal after she had unpacked; she had a myriad of tales to tell about different boys and girls that she met. Out she blurted, "Momma, did you know that there is a pill that you can take to keep you from getting pregnant when you have sex?". Just imagine my thoughts. Here I was over 55 years old with 10 children under my belt and my teenager was telling me about birth control! I showed no expression and asked, "How does it work?" To my astonishment she answered! She said that some boy had explained that all the girls use it; you just take it with water or milk or juice everyday and you can have sex without getting pregnant.

Now needless to say I was amazed! I still showed no expression and replied, "No, I never heard of that. Did you try it?" "No", she replied. I looked at her and very calmly said, "Well good. You know you should never have sex before marriage; when you do get married your love for your husband will make sex have meaning. Then when you have children it will be because you both want to have a family, not because you were careless and irresponsible with your gift to him." "I know Mom", she said and just walked off just as nonchalant like we had just talked about the weather! Meanwhile, I was silently thanking God that he had spared me a heart attack. When she left the room I said, "Whew!" I never told Joann how proud I was that she did not *follow the crowd*. I remembered the scripture that says that you train children up in the way they should go and when they are old they will not depart from it. She could have easily taken the pill and begun sexual promiscuity and I might never have known it. But she never forgot her upbringing—the moral values that I had taught her and that she saw in me. And because I kept an open mind and an open line of communication with her she openly discussed this very important issue with me.

Lesson Five: If you receive a letter from the college make sure you understand its meaning, *otherwise known as if your* *child' college sends you a letter containing the words all night parietal, it's probably best to check it out, just for clarification.* Remember the story of the trip Peggie and I took to Smith. We had driven from Baltimore to Northampton without incident; both of us were so glad that we had finally arrived. Remember how open minded I had become thanks to her older sister, Joann. I thought I had just about seen and heard everything; after all Bennie had brought hippie friends home from MIT, Joann had brought her boyfriend home from Mercer with her several times to stay, and Peggie had brought three of her girlfriends home with her during Spring Break as they traveled from New York to Birmingham to Atlanta and back to Smith in a rental car. I had heard a thousand tales from Enoch, Bennie, Joann, and Peggie about their adventures away from home; I watched them all enjoy life and yet adhere to the values that were engrained in them from childhood. I had never been worried or concerned as they flew to locations all over the United States to work or participate in programs during the summers while they were in school. They had enjoyed a proper upbringing of which Enoch and I were proud.

Well soon after we parked in the Quad two boys jumped out of a car behind us to help with our luggage. One of the boys was her boyfriend; the other was a mutual friend and the boy's roommate. They were well groomed and mannerable. We were introduced and they grabbed the bags as we started into Gardiner House where she stayed. I noticed that this child of mine kept saying "Mom, now don't be surprised at anything you see". I wondered, "Why is she telling me this?" We entered Gardiner House a building that reminded me of the beautiful old English mansions you see in magazines. The main floor was absolutely exquisite; period rugs and runners were in place so that as you walked your feet never touched the beautiful hardwood floors that shined and sparkled beneath. Ornate chandeliers adorned the foyer and the hallways. To the right was a stunning living room complete with various period sofas and chairs, along-with solid cherry tables and accompanying lamps. The dining room was filled with beautiful cherry dining room tables, china, and silver, with crystal and white linen napkins. White cooks prepared the meals and White housekeepers maintained the premises. Imagine my surprise after having been in situations where blacks always held such positions!

My child was completely oblivious to my comments; after all, this magnificent place had been her home away from home for the past three years. It was as common to her as any other aspect of her life; she befriended girls who had maids and butlers as well as girls who lived in homes like hers. She was comfortable in the environment and I was so proud that she had the opportunity to experience it all. Anyway while I was "Oooh-ing" and "Aaah-ing" about the house she just kept telling me that her room was on the second floor. As I began to walk up the stairs I noticed that my daughter started again, "Mom, please don't say anything—no matter what you see"; she mumbled this over and over the entire time that I walked up the stairs. The boys that were walking right in front of us, looked at each other and smiled sheepishly. I saw why—there were boys running around in pajamas going in and out of girls' rooms, into the restroom, out of the rest room in towels, and I said to myself, "What is going on here?" When I got to her room I was about to do the 20-question routine when another girl, a friend of hers named Carol, came in the room and introduced herself. That weekend was the longest one of my life—I saw college life at it's finest!

Well I survived and adjusted to the resident life at Smith College. I met some wonderful young ladies and young men, all of whom were very well mannered. I enjoyed delicious meals in the dining room and had a ball visiting the various sites around town. Northampton was a true college town and Peggie took me over to the other area colleges (UMASS,

Amherst, and Holyoke) to give me a feel for her life away from home. The girls went to a party that night at UMASS the school where Peggie's boyfriend attended. I don't remember what time she came in; the next day Peggie and Carol drove me to the airport at Hartford, Connecticut. Carol threw up in the back seat while we were in route; I never knew if it was from drinking too much at the party the night before or from the jerky drive (the Volkswagen was a stick shift and Peggie was still learning how to change the gears!). At that point I did not dare ask; I did not want to know! I flew back home out of Hartford that Sunday and prayed the whole way home. I did not pray because of the flight—it was smooth; I prayed because my baby had been in an environment with so much freedom all those years and I did not know it. I thanked God for keeping her safe . . . . and for not allowing me to know it until it was too late! Later as I recalled this incident Peggie reminded me that I had received a letter in the mail that explained the college's position on overnight *parietal* (for friends of the opposite sex). I smiled because I remembered receiving the letter. I did not know the meaning of the word but I trusted in God and her so much that I did not even look the word up in the dictionary. Smith College was and still is a fine all girls' Ivy League school. And my baby girl is all the more educated, polished, and experienced—able to meet the challenges of this old world head on—because of having been there!

Lesson Six: A break for them is not a break for you, *otherwise known as there is no such thing as a break from being a parent.* I always looked forward to breaks that the children had over the years. At first they came home for Thanksgiving, Christmas, and Spring Break. As they befriended other children they either went home with them or brought them to our house. Now each child handled the breaks differently. Joann usually brought her boyfriend or her best friend Quintress home with her for a break; she would return the kindness to them the next break. She was very social and very popular so even though she had a boyfriend at school she had other boys who would come over to see her as soon as she got home. Joann's dresses appeared to shrink in size during these visits—it never ceased to amaze me how this child could look so innocent and yet be so alluring. I trusted her but watched her like a hawk!

Now you would think that while they were away they would wash their clothes. NO SUCH LUCK! Bennie was the world's worse! He would save all of his dirty laundry from the whole semester (not really, but sure seemed like it) and bring it home for ME to wash! On top of that it was nothing for him to have several old high school friends come and visit while he was home—not to mention the friends he brought home with him (in route to their homes). Now of course Enoch and I were expected to provide food and drink for these young people so that Bennie and his guests were treated well. And so we did.

Peggie would either go to visit her favorite big sister Grace, spend a week with Irene during Thanksgiving and Spring Break, or visit with friends. At Christmas she had the longest break of them all—she was home from the week before Christmas to almost the end of January because of the snowfall in Northampton. Needless to say she wanted special food, her clothes had to be washed, and she had to call her friends all over the country! Mom, the substitute Maid (that's me), was supposed to take care of all the cooking, dish washing, linen, etc. And of course she also was quite the socialite who was visited by friends, old and new (male and female), while she was "*in town*"!

Well as much as I loved and missed these children these breaks of theirs were *killing* me! I kept praying, "Lord let them hurry up and graduate so that they can get out on their own!" He answered my prayers all too soon. I really missed them when they went off to different parts of the country to work. And let me tell you I would not exchange one minute of the time that I spent catering to them and their friends over the years for anything else. They have all repaid me 10 times over with gifts of money, jewelry, trips, and clothes—anything I have ever wanted my children have given me. It reminds me of the old saying, *"Cast your bread upon the water and it will return to you ten-fold"*. It was great being the recipient of so many expressions of gratitude and love; but the most important benefit was that they shared so much of their lives with me. I learned so much through them and we became so very close!

Why are these lessons important? For one thing parents today are so busy that they seldom take the time to really learn from their children. In order to learn any lesson you have to pay attention to the details. That means caring for and taking care of your children, which includes listening and paying attention to them—to what is important to *them*! It is only when children feel like you will listen without condemnation that they will begin to share their dreams, their fears, their triumphs, their failures—their *lives* with you. And who knows you may even learn something new! Imagine that! Your child might be able to teach YOU something! If you never learn that effective communication includes listening you will miss out on the most valuable part of being a parent. Because I was always a good listener and one who believed in allowing my children to experience things on their own they were never afraid to openly share the major incidents in their lives with me; and since I remained open-minded they tended to ask me for advice. Yes, it is possible that your children will actually ASK YOU for advice! I am 88 years old and my children still come to me for advice before major decisions are made; they still value my opinion. I have had many young people tell me that they wished that I had been their Mother. And I have always been asked to talk about (and have always enjoyed sharing) my ideas on parenting with others. One such time in particular will always be remembered.

During the time that my younger children were in high

school Enoch's youngest sister Julia worked with a Dr. Martha McCranie; Dr. McCranie was a psychiatrist at the Medical College of Georgia who held a lot of seminars and lectures in the community on child psychiatry and child rearing. Dr. McCranie was very involved in child advocacy programs. Her daughter was attending Richmond Academy and told her about a "brilliant and friendly" female in her class; that female was my daughter, Joann. Dr. McCranie later wrote:

> "Sometime in the mid nineteen sixties I became aware there was an unusual family somewhere in East Augusta. My daughter at Augusta's Richmond Academy, told me of a brilliant and friendly fellow female student who had taken advantage of the Freedom of Choice policy where a person from a Black School could attend the supposedly better White School of his or her choice. Joann Ward entered ARC."

When Dr. McCranie mentioned the name *Joann Ward,* Julia told her that Joann was one of her nieces. Julia arranged for Dr. McCranie to come to my house to meet me. Of that visit Dr. McCranie wrote:

> "Mrs. Ward allowed me to visit in her home. A neat house in a well-kept neighborhood near East Boundary. The clutter of books, papers, typewriters gave evidence of the family's interest and involvement in scholarly activity. I understood there were other children in the family—and from time to time heard of their notable achievements."

Dr. McCranie had been asked to speak at a local PTA meeting on child rearing; she asked me and two other mothers to participate in a panel discussion as "examples illustrating to the group some factors in successful child rearing". "Mrs. Ward exemplified a dedicated successful mother, confident and happy in her role", she wrote.

We were asked to discuss the key factors for successful parenting, which to me was the same as telling the group how my ten children were brought up. There were three major topics that the panel addressed. They were:

1. Respect of each parent for the other.
2. Recognizing the adult's place in the family as different from the child's place
3. Exposing the child to the tools and ways needed to be successful in society.

To address these issues I explained how my husband was the head of our household. I told them how he worked and that I stayed at home, assuming the role of wife and mother to the children. I said that we taught our children by our example through the lives that we lived before them. I told them that the children were introduced to Jesus Christ and the Church at an early age, which became the basis for their upbringing. From that basis they learned all about love, obedience, honor, and respect—the key ingredients to success. I explained myself further by telling them that Church (God) is the secret to bringing up a good child.

First, I talked about how I fulfilled my obligation as a Christian Mother by teaching and training them to obey God's laws. If they obeyed God's laws they wouldn't have any problems with laws made by man. I explained how I taught them about Jesus Christ and how they should follow his example, always attempting to do what is right. I took them to Church and fulfilled my obligation to train them up in the admonition of God. I did not have to spank my children often because we taught them early on the right way. But when they did something wrong I spanked them right then. I told them that you could spank a child with words, too; it does not always have to be with your hand or a belt.

Next I discussed how my children saw Enoch and me respect each other; we respected them so they respected us. We told our children to respect others if they wanted to be respected; they were reminded of the golden rule: *"Do unto others as you would have others do unto you"*. We knew that we had 10 children and that they were all different. We accepted each child as a unique part of the family; they knew that there was a special place in our hearts, a place that belonged only to them, for each one.

Then I explained how I fulfilled my obligations to them as the Mother in the family. I got up every morning to make sure that they had a warm breakfast so that they did not go to school on an empty stomach; children learn better when they are not hungry. And when they came home after school I was there waiting with a warm hot dinner that was a balanced meal to nourish them. They always had clean clothes to wear every day because I washed and ironed them. They went to school spiritually, emotionally, mentally and physically ready to learn.

My children knew that they could come home to me (and their Dad) and confide in us; they were taught that their home was a safe-haven. I always listened to what they had to say; you learn a whole lot more when you listen than if you're always talking or not paying attention to what's important to them. We taught them to pick their company; we opened the doors of our home to their friends. I did not have to worry about who they spent time with because I knew the kids. They came to my house to play music, study, eat, or just to sit and talk. I told the audience that I taught my children to share and to cast their bread upon the water so that it would return to them ten-fold.

My children were always encouraged to do their best. I told the audience about how I had always taught my children to be careful and to take care of everything. I also explained how important it is to communicate with the school and to let the children know that you are communicating. I stayed in touch with the school and was involved in the PTA. I told them about the sibling pressure and that God blessed me with ten children who were taught to love, look after, and help each other; this led them to achieve and to become self-motivated. Finally I explained that all of our teaching was by example; parents must lead by example. My children never saw my husband and me fighting or working against each other; we always worked together. The children always saw us worship God; they always saw us giving and sharing. They saw me constantly reading and writing and trying to learn. They watched as I set goals for my home and my family and observed how I worked diligently and steadfastly, with their Father, to achieve those goals. And they saw Enoch and me do all the things that we expected of them. They loved us and they knew that we loved them. From the day that they were born I rarely left them; Enoch and I took the kids with us almost everywhere. I took care of and was careful with the tiniest of things, which carried over to them and caused them to excel. I told that audience that I was so proud of them all.

The audience gave me a big round of applause that evening. Julia was in the audience and she clapped, too. "Sister Renie, you were so good!", she said. Afterwards, I was told that the speech was filmed and that an excerpt would be aired on television and put in the local paper. Now I wish I had kept the clipping; but it's all right. I look at my children and all that they have done—that's my proof that I have been a successful Mother.

The theme of that group meeting was "A Mother's Job is to Work Herself out of a Job". Dr. McCranie later said that I was a *perfect model*. And you know she was right; I was the perfect model of a Mother who had worked herself right out of a job. When Peggie graduated in 1974 from Smith College, Enoch and I were left with each other. My oldest son J.E. worked for a contractor in Augusta and was out on his own. Charles had made Los Angeles his home and had gone back to school using the GI Bill and received B.S. and Masters degrees in electrical engineering from the University of California; he was a successful engineer for Rockwell International and Northrop. Lee Mark had moved to Los Angeles, spent a year in the Army, got a degree in business, and began working for the US Postal Service. Grace had a degree in English from Paine College and a Masters degree in English & Journalism from Johns Hopkins University and was working as a Senior Teacher. Irene had received her business degree from Queens College in New York and was a successful director of hospital administration. Katherine had a degree in elementary education from Paine College and was an accomplished middle school teacher for the state of New Jersey. Enoch, Jr. had a Chemical Engineering degree from Georgia Tech and had become a Vice President for Proctor & Gamble. Bennie had B.S. degrees in Math and Physics from MIT and Masters and Ph.D. degrees in Physics from Princeton University; he was a successful research Nuclear Physicist and Professor. Joann had received her degree in Math from Mercer University; she was a successful electrical engineer. Peggie had received her Bachelor's degree in Math from Smith College; she was off to graduate school at Georgia Tech.

Imagine how I felt after being on a job for 42 years to wake up suddenly unemployed! You would think that we could relax and enjoy the rest of our years because all of our children were independent and had been successful in achieving their professional and personal goals. In truth we were lonely and glad when our children and grandchildren came to visit, which was far more frequent than we expected. We loved and looked forward to every visit!

Ain't Life Grand

Every parent looks forward to the day that their children are grown, self-sufficient, productive citizens who are out on their own. As with most families my children achieved this independence at varying times depending on the individual personality of each child. I always told the bird story—you've heard it a million times. It goes like this. "See how the Mother bird gently pushes her baby out of the nest to coach him to fly? She stays close by to watch what he does and to make sure he's safe. The little bird tries and if he fails, the Mother comes and gets him; she nurtures him and encourages him to try again. Eventually, the bird takes off and stays in flight. He flies short distances from the nest at first, returning to Mother for support and further instruction. Finally, when he is confident he takes off and goes out on his own." Now you should start this story while the child is young, preferably while you are actually watching the birds go through this process with their young ones. You follow the story with, "See, that's what you are going to do, too, when you grow up". If this doesn't sink in by the time the child is 30 don't panic. You just have to be firm and ask him very directly: "When are you planning on flying?"

Regardless of method used eventually most children get the message and venture out on their own to start their own nest, baby birds included. One of the best parts of the process is that they return with their children for (hopefully) short visits so that you enjoy participating in the upbringing of your grandchildren. Nothing is funnier than watching your children try to get their children to conform to rules that you had difficulty getting them to follow. When one of my children complained about a character trait in a child my pat answer was, "You reap what you sow!". They always looked at me in dismay; that was not exactly the answer they expected. Of course I would always follow with more advice; but I truly enjoyed being able to give that little reminder, especially to one of my boys.

You would think that I would have had 50 grand children; no such luck! I had eight—Edwina, Julius, Kenneth, Kevin, Tamara, Kiffiny, Justin, and Jaime. I thought all of my grandchildren were just adorable. Edwina was James' only child. She was a very fair skinned child with long hair; she loved her "Grand Mama", as she would affectionately call me. Now parents expect that their children will be jealous of their siblings but not their nieces or nephews. Since Peggie was only a few years older than Edwina, she felt very threatened by her. Whenever I called J.E. and Thelma to make arrangements to keep her Peggie would have a fit! "Mom, don't go and get her; let her stay at home", she would whine. I would end up placing Peggie on one knee and Edwina on the other. As the years went by the two girls became very close and learned to love each other. As young children they both wanted my undivided attention; I enjoyed every minute of being in that kind of demand!

Lee Mark and his wife Gailey had two boys, Julius and Kenneth. When the couple started out the family lived in Compton. Lee Mark became concerned about the boys being left at home while they were at work. He was not concerned about the family who would keep the children (it was his wife's family)—but that his two boys might not have the benefit of the value system he had been taught as a child if they associated with children outside of the family circle. He asked me if I would keep the two boys for a while until he and his wife got situated. Enoch and I discussed it and agreed to keep the two boys for a while; we did not actually place a time limit on their stay. The two children stayed with us as toddlers for over a year; the youngest called me "MA", which he pronounced with a "w" as "Maw". Bennie would hear him and promptly say, "Boy, that's not your Mother; that's my Mother!" Kenny would look so pitiful that I would grab him and hug him. I felt so sorry for him; I could not believe that his Mother would willingly leave such a young child. I realize now that she was too young to know any better. Kenny was always a slow talker and not as quick on his feet as his older brother. I would watch the two of them; the oldest was very smart and strong-willed so the young one would cling to him for support and help. Julius had a photographic memory like me. He also had the city slick ways of a Californian; he was a challenge but I made a difference in both their little lives. That little Julius could look at a book and memorize every word or picture he saw, reciting it flawlessly upon request. At the age of 3 he could also out curse a sailor. It took me a while but I cleaned up his language and taught him two new words—"No" and "Obey"! About the time that I had these two youngsters in control, Billy and Gailey came back to collect them. They never stayed with me again; I would see them during visits and talk to them frequently on the phone. My grandsons in California always had a special place in our hearts.

After these two boys my little Enoch's boy, Kevin, was born. He was very fair skinned like his Mother with features like his Dad. I practically reared him since for most of his formative years he stayed with me off and on. When Kevin was in daycare Mrs. Mitchell would often call me to tell me that Enoch and Gloria had dropped him off at the Church and that he was sick. Sometimes she would call Enoch Jr., who would bring him to me to "*keep*" for the rest of the day; at other times she would bring him directly to me. As soon as Kevin got settled I would ask, "Kev, what's wrong?" He would of course say he didn't feel good. I would go into the kitchen and fix him a warm hot breakfast. He would eat and in an hour or so be ready to play. He would stay around the house and play most of the day as he told me all about my son's (and my son's wife's) affairs. I would just listen; I learned more about what was going on in their household from Kevin than Enoch. Jr. or Gloria would care to tell!

Now when Peggie was young she had a head full of thick long hair. I had not seen a child with as much hair until I saw Grace's daughter, Tammy; she had more hair than any little girl I had ever seen. I never will forget the first time I saw her as a toddler. Grace had her all dressed up in the cutest little dress and shoes; her hair was combed out in a big Afro style. I actually thought the child's head would make her fall; she looked too tiny to carry around all that hair! Tammy had inherited her Dad's frugal nature; I remember being out to lunch with them. Justin was there and Tammy asked, "If you had a choice between a quarter and a piece of candy, which would you choose?" Justin was younger and said, "The candy". Tammy quickly explained to her younger cousin that he was wrong; he should choose the quarter because if he saved enough of them, he could buy as much candy as he wanted. I thought to myself that this little girl would have a good financial head on her shoulders; and she has done just that!

Kiffiny was born when Enoch, Jr. and Gloria were living in Maryland; Enoch, Jr. was a Vice President for Proctor and Gamble. Gloria came back and forth to Augusta to her doctor for office visits; she wanted her baby to be born here in Augusta near her Mom. Kiffiny was a cute little baby but mean as all get out! I never will forget the first time that I kept her; she cried constantly! She wanted her Mom and no person or thing, not even her Dad, could stop her from crying! I always loved her but she was so very close to her Mom that I seldom kept her in my care like the others. She and her Mom are still close. It reminds me of the closeness that I have with my baby, Peggie. When she was young she never wanted to leave my side. When she got older she wanted to live everywhere—and she thought I should just tag along for the ride—to keep her company. I did just that for many years. Whenever she has needed me I have tried to be there for her, just as I have been for all the other children. And now she is the only one of my girls near me; I am so glad that we were always close because I don't know what I would do without her!

Peggie had lived in Massachusetts, Georgia, Ohio, and California. She moved back to Augusta, got married, and had Justin. She stayed home with the baby for several months before she went back to work at a job almost 60 miles from where she lived. It was difficult for her to get back to a daycare before it closed so I agreed to keep little Justin while she worked. My grandchildren all loved me but this child had a special place in our hearts, as Peggie had in my Dad's heart. When she was a small child my Dad would catch a ride with the Postal carrier to my house; when we looked up he was at the front door. He would always bring Peggie her favorite treat, one of those little Coca Cola's. Dad would sit there telling her one story after another, laughing and talking as they shared that soda. She loved him so much; theirs was a special relationship, as was ours with Justin.

In fact this child called me "Ganny" for Granny. If he wanted something or needed help he would come to his Ganny. Enoch loved him so much that he would give him a dollar every time he saw him. Now Justin did not realize it but he was accumulating quite a sum of money. He was adorable (I say that all my grand's are adorable). He had weighed only 4 pounds and 12 ounces at birth; thanks to my old-fashioned feeding methods I had him weighing in at over 13 pounds in just 12 weeks! Today he is over six feet tall and weighs in at well over 200 pounds. In recent years, Justin has picked me up, holding me ever so gently in much the same way that I used to hold him. Justin will always hold a special place in my heart.

Jaime, the last of my grandchildren, was born 7 months after Justin. My daughter Irene and her husband, William, lived in New York during Jaime's childhood. When she was younger Irene would make sure that I got to see her at least once a year. We would play checkers and have the best talks; she would tell me her concerns about her older Mother. Irene was 41 when she had Jaime just as I had been 40 when I had Peggie; the difference was that Jaime was Irene's first and only child. Quite naturally she was protective because she loved her so much. I would tell her not to worry; in time her Mother would get more used to the idea that she had to let go. She would hug and kiss me and thank me for listening to her. I always tried to encourage my children and my grandchildren. And Jaime made sure that she wrote me and called me to keep me abreast of the major issues in her life. Jaime also has turned out to be a fine young woman.

In case you haven't noticed, I am a proud grandmother, too! My grandchildren who grew up around me have reaped the direct benefit of my attention, love, and guidance. I have been able to influence their thinking and their behavior in a positive way. And those who are far away have been influenced as well. You see I look at my grandchildren and see that my children have imparted to them the same morals and values that I taught them. I still remember them at Christmas and on Birthday's and I take advantage of every opportunity to show them how much I love them. I have had private little talks with them when they needed someone other than Mom or Dad to talk to; and I have secretly taken issues to their parents on their behalf—lobbying for them and their right to be their own persons. I have prayed with them, prayed for them, played with them, disciplined them and cuddled them. It's been grand to have grand's!

My Utmost

You know Enoch and I always gave our utmost to God and to our children. During the entire time that we were bringing up our children we continued to attend Church, pay our tithes, and to work together as a family unit to give our children all that we had to support their efforts. We prayed for our children that God would lead and guide them towards the right way. We asked Him to protect them. They watched us make sacrifices. In fact except by the grace of God I can't really explain how they were able to do many of the things that they accomplished. They flew on airplanes, ate in the finest restaurants, traveled, and experienced many things that they would never have been exposed to had they stayed in Augusta. They certainly could not rely on their Dad or me to help them very much financially; we gave them all that we could but most importantly they helped each other and themselves. In their hearts they knew we were here for the kinds of things money can't buy—love, support, encouragement, advice, a hug, and a kiss. And I have always felt gratified as I watched them with each other and their own families; it is so obvious that they have followed our example. There are so many wonderful stories to tell. I have already shared several of my favorites. Here's another. You know flying on an airplane was expensive. So unless a black person was wealthy, in the military, or worked for the airlines, s/he took the bus, the train, or drove a car to places out of town.

Well shortly after Peggie graduated from Smith College Charles got married. He purchased tickets for Peggie, his Father and me to fly out to the wedding, so we did. Now I had flown out to California in 1972 for my 60th birthday; Enoch had never flown on a plane before but was finally convinced that it was safe. Peggie had flown back and forth to school several times each year; she thought flying was the only way to travel! Anyway we finally got Enoch to agree to go.

California (which by the way back then was synonymous to LA as far as I was concerned) was one of my favorite places to visit because of the differences in life styles. There was a Church on every corner and a liquor store across the street. Back then most of the common black folks lived in LA, Compton (a suburb of Watts!), or Lynn. It was nothing for you to see people dressed in a fur coat and driving a Rolls Royce to the grocery store. I expected that of the movie stars but the black folks that lived in downtown LA in what looked like houses in poor Southern neighborhoods often were the folks with the furs and fancy cars. My children would whisper, "drug money" in my ear. And yes, I came to understand what that truly meant in the years to follow. However, even on reflection it is difficult for me to understand why someone would place material things such as clothes or a car at a higher priority than his family or home. "Upbringing", would always be my staunch reply and I was right.

My attitude was a result of the fact that when I was a child my parents made our home (and family) the center of most family activities. We worshipped God, learned how to love, and how to live at home. When money and those things replace values in a home a spiritual, emotional, and moral breakdown occurs. That's what has happened to many American families. I look back at our lives and our meager beginnings; back then we had far less material things and money than we have now but our lives were so rich. Even while we were in California Bennie was remodeling and bricking our home of over 20 years. Why? Because when he offered to buy us a nicer bigger home we refused. Instead we told him what we would like to have done to make our existing home nicer. You see our home was the place where we lived and loved; it was our most precious possession on earth. Outside of God and family, it had been the central focus of our lives—and no car, fur, or any other measure of wealth was more defining than the place we called home.

When I looked at some of the black people in Los Angeles I thought they had it all wrong; their priorities were in all the wrong places. They had free education yet very few of them took advantage of it and went to school. They had money to invest in a car or fur or diamonds but they did not realize that an investment in home, land, and an education would give returns for the long term—returns that could be passed down from generation to generation. Back then I thought that everything looked big and new in Los Angeles; today now that Augusta has grown so much many of the places in Los Angeles look old.

Hollywood was something to see back then. I loved Lucille Ball, Redd Foxx, Red Skelton, Dinah Shore, and the other stars; so naturally I wanted to take the bus tour to see the Movie Stars' homes and other tourist attractions everywhere. Today if I want to see a fabulous home I can just visit one of my kids! Anyway Peggie had to go to Disneyland and Universal Studios. Eating out in a real Mexican restaurant was another one of our favorite things to do. Enoch did not want to do anything; the kids took Peggie and me while he stayed home and rested. Charles and Cheryl had a beautiful wedding; and my daughter-in-law's family was as nice as they could be to all of us. Despite all the fun and nice treatment, when we got back home to Augusta Enoch quickly advised me that he would never fly again—and he didn't!

In 1976 Peggie accepted a job in Ohio working for General Motors. Her favorite brother Bennie was just a couple of hours away in Indiana; he was a Physics professor at Purdue University in West Lafayette. He came home for a visit and she followed him to her new home; as usual *"Ma Maid"* (that's me) went along for the ride. It was my first visit to Ohio; the people and countryside reminded me somewhat of home. Peggie had lived there during a summer as a General Motors Scholar working at the Dayton Data Center; she knew her way around so we ate in a nice restaurant and reserved a room in a hotel for the first night. Bennie drove on up to West Lafayette after dinner. The next morning we quickly got an apartment for her and visited furniture stores and the Dayton Mall to get housekeeping basics. We met the Jones', a family who had been very hospitable to her during her stay in the summer; we also enjoyed fine dining and shopping. Her furniture was not to be delivered until Monday so we slept on the floor. Now I was almost 64 years old so my bones were *crying out* to me by morning. I kissed her, hugged her, and flew back home the next day right after breakfast! I thanked God for the safe trip and having a bed to sleep on when I returned.

Five years later in 1981 the children held a 50th Wedding Anniversary for Enoch and me. The entire time that each child was in school they would always ask, "Mom, you all have been good to me, what do you want me to do for you when I graduate?" My response would always be the same; I wanted to have a 50th wedding anniversary to renew our vows with friends, neighbors, Clarks, and Ward's as witnesses. On the first Saturday in June 1981, my children made that dream come true at the Hilton Hotel downtown. The celebration was held in grand style. The children rented a room for the ceremony, a banquet room for a reception (featuring a sit-down meal at tables outfitted with white linen tablecloths, china, silver, and service), and a separate area for dancing. I had on a beautiful wedding gown with a veil and a long train; Enoch had on a tuxedo. All of the children (except Irene and J.E.) participated. My girls were my bridesmaids (all dressed in white long gowns) and the boys were all dressed in tuxedos as Enoch's groomsmen. My oldest grandson Julius put on James' tuxedo and took his place in the lineup. We were escorted from our house to the affair by limousine. While Enoch and I wished that all the children had been able to participate we refused to let anything spoil the day for us.

Rev. N. T. Young led us through a beautiful ceremony in a room decorated with flowers and candles where Enoch and I renewed our vows. We ate dinner in the banquet room, after which we cut a beautiful three-tiered wedding cake. My sisters, brothers, and their families came from Millen, Savannah, Detroit, and all over the country; my children came from Baltimore, Los Angeles, and San Francisco. Friends from my childhood, our Church members, neighbors, and the friends of my children all attended. During the reception we all danced and socialized as my son-in-law played the most beautiful music. It was a dream come true; I had not been happier in a very long time. It was truly a gala affair!

In the years to come the other children would migrate back and forth between Los Angeles, other states in the nation, and home—visiting each other and us as often as possible. The next year Peggie went out to LaJolla Beach, California on her job. We stopped over in Los Angeles at Disneyland so that her two and a half year old son could see the theme park and I could visit with my children. I had thought that the most scenic place in California was LA and the surrounding areas until I saw LaJolla Beach. We stayed in a hotel right on the beach where you could see the ocean from the bedroom windows; it was like waking up in a postcard! We took the baby to the San Diego Zoo; it was a wonderful trip. My grandson, Justin, loved to fly; at two years old he had experienced something that my Father would have loved to experience but never did! I watched and marveled as he played and laughed on the large plane thinking how far we had come. "We had reached for the sky Dad", I thought, "and touched it!"

Eleven years after Charles' wedding and just 4 years after Julius had been a groomsman at our anniversary he was killed. Peggie, her little boy Justin, and I made the long trip to LA again; I was 73. However, this time there would be no celebration. Julius, Lee Mark's oldest son, had gotten involved in a moneymaking scheme that had gone bad. As I sat there at the funeral I wondered what *Kenny* would do without his older brother. And I wondered if my grandson's fate would have been different if I had continued to keep him in Augusta. Of course I will never know; it just seemed such a shame for such a young life with so much potential to end so early. Julius was so well known and loved by the youth in the city that there was a line of mourners that extended for blocks down and around the sides of the church; there were more than a hundred young people who came to pay respect to this special young man. He was buried in Forest Lawn Cemetery. The lives of my son, his wife, and their youngest child were forever changed by this senseless act.

The next time I flew to LA I was in route to Hawaii. Yes, that's right! My oldest girl Grace and her husband, Gray, gave me a trip to Hawaii as a 75th birthday present. It was the most beautiful place that I had ever been. I love flowers; the flowers in Hawaii were the most beautiful I had ever seen. As I looked at them they were so different I thought of Adam and Eve and the Garden of Eden. It was breathtaking! The water was so blue and clear. Grace and Tammy, my granddaughter, were there with me; Grace had purchased a tourist package that included the roasted pig birthday luau, a trip 10,000 feet to the top of a volcano, flights to all of the major islands, a tour of Pearl Harbor, and more. Peggie had bought me the cutest skirted bathing suit and I played in the ocean and enjoyed the clear white sandy beaches. I had the time of my life; I still wear the charm around my neck with the word *Hawaii* etched in gold; it is a constant reminder of my visit to Hawaii.

My happiness quickly ended when I came back to find my husband dehydrated and completely under nourished. Enoch had been invited to go with me to Hawaii but had refused. Peggie, J.E., and Enoch, Jr. had convinced me that they would come to the house to make sure he had plenty of warm food to eat; they said that they would make sure that he was cared for on a daily basis. He refused to let them care for him and often times would not eat; he was lost without me. The Sunday after my return we were on our way to Church with Peggie when her Dad's nose started to bleed profusely. She got an ice pack, applied ice and pressure, and had him hold his nose back; still his nose bled. Without saying a word she headed to the hospital. He was admitted immediately; the nosebleed was a result of more serious internal bleeding due to polyps and an ulcerated stomach condition. He was fed intravenously for a day or so; as soon as he got a little better he decided he was coming home. He got up in the middle of the night, popped the IV needle from his arm, and headed towards the elevator leaving a trail of blood. The Nurse stopped him, put him back in bed and called me. The next day the doctor agreed to allow him to come home.

The next several years were quietly spent at home. I took care of my husband and spent time helping my daughter Peggie with her son, Justin. He had just turned 5 when Julius died; it was the first funeral he had ever attended. I will never forget how moving it was when he reached into the casket and touched Julius' face; Peggie and I wept. This little boy's Mother and Father had a turbulent marriage. After my daughter divorced her husband of 8 years she

befriended the White man whom she married after 3 years
of courtship. My sisters and several of the family members
attended the wedding. I worried about the marriage because
of the racial differences and the times in which we lived;
and I worried about little Justin, too. Justin grew up to be a
fine young man with wonderful values largely because of
the closeness of our family and the influence of this white
man. He adopted Justin (giving him his last name) and
brought him up as his own. It reminded me so much of
what my Dad did for my Mother with my older sister. Wayne's
own children and family disowned him because he married
a black woman. I want them all to know that Wayne became
a part of a family full of values, culture, and pride. He could
not have done better—bar none, black or white.

Over the years I have become so attached to my son-in-
law that the color lines that were once so clearly drawn for
me during my childhood have begun to fade. Wayne is and
has been a true *son* to both Enoch and me. When I think
about the racial division that still exists in the world it saddens
my heart. How can a person be a true Christian and be a
racist? All people need to look at themselves and realize
that God made them in His own image. Everybody in the
world should think about that God loves the white, the black,
the poor, the rich, the fortunate, the unfortunate, the sick,
the healthy, the crippled, the blind, the ugly, the pretty, the
deaf, the dumb, the smart, the gifted, the talented, and the
untalented. Everything and everybody belongs to God. And
if people would just read the Bible—it has not changed! If
we read it, trust it, and believe in what it says, it will help us
to stay on the right path. For it contains the word of God—
a guide for all mankind. In it you will find:

> *The state of man, the way of salvation*
> *The doom of sinners, and happiness for believers*
> *Its doctrine is holy, its precepts are binding*
> *Its histories are true and its discussions are immutable*

Read it to be wise, believe it to be safe and practice it to be holy
For it contains a light to direct your path, food to support
*   you*
And comfort to cheer you.
It's the traveler's map, the Pilgrim's staff, and the Soldier's
*   sword.*
It is the Christian Charter; Paradise is restarted.
Heaven will be open to you and the gates of hell will be closed.

For His Highest

My older sister attended Peggie's wedding. She knew how much it would mean for her to be there—not just to Peggie but also to me. That was in October; she had a stroke during the Christmas holidays of that same year and went into a catatonic state. She was alive; her eyes would open but she could not talk or move. Her children spared no expense to get her the very best of medical attention; nothing changed her condition. My sister who loved to talk, sing, eat, and travel was bedridden and had to be fed intravenously. I remembered the time that we talked about her being sick and going into a hospital when we were just children in the outhouse. Over the past 50 years of my life she had been in the hospital time after time with one ailment after another; but she had always bounced back—as if nothing would ever really deter her course. She would visit all of our sisters and brothers who lived far away and come back to give all of us here at home a full report. In fact it had not been all that long ago that she had spent the night with me. I remember that I fried some Brim and made a sweet potato pie, some cornbread, and collard greens. We ate and talked all evening long. The next day her baby girl came by to carry her back home. It was so difficult for me to bear seeing her in her condition; it was as if her premonition came true. I know that God in his infinite wisdom makes no mistakes but I could not comprehend it.

The first time I went to see my sister she made a noise repeatedly as if to say, "Hello, I know you're here". I would grab her hand and she would settle down. I know that her children noticed that I made seldom visits to see my favorite sister; if only they knew how my heart was broken each time I saw her like that. We were too close—I loved her too much to see her that way! No, I preferred to remember my sister as the lively socialite—my best friend with whom I could talk for hours—tirelessly living life to the fullest! When I see her in heaven what a reunion it will be!

As the months went by I became more and more depressed about my sister. The children knew how I felt about her, especially Peggie. They decided that it was about time for another celebration—something to cheer me up! All of the children collaborated to give me a gala 80th birthday celebration on July 5th, 1992, at the Sheraton Hotel off Wheeler Road. Peggie took care of the details since she was here. It was beautifully done; the color scheme was ivory & rose. Peggie had a tailor make the two of us beautiful coordinating rose-colored satin dresses. She had programs printed and souvenir matchbooks and napkins made. There was a sit-down meal at round tables adorned with white linen tablecloths, silver, and service. The menu consisted of a choice of three different entrees, side dishes, salad, a variety of breads, ice tea, a birthday cake, and champagne. A live band played music while we ate and for dancing after the meal. The children presented me with $1,000 plus a beautiful 11x14 portrait. A professional photographer was contracted to capture the entire event on film; I still have the album with all the pictures and a video of my 80th birthday party. All of my children and their children were there except J.E. He had promised that he would come but never showed up. Each child had a part in the program; it touched my heart to know that all of them loved me as much as I loved them. I know that J.E. knew that we all loved him but he made himself feel inferior by always comparing himself to the others. All of my sisters and brothers who were in the area from Savannah and Millen came to my birthday party—my friends and neighbors came, too. It was a very special occasion that I will never forget.

Enoch was 86 and his health was failing so Enoch, Jr. took his Father's place as my partner during the first dance. My husband sat there largely unaware of what was happening. Katherine would later tell us that she had dropped by to see her Dad and me before the affair. She would recall that her Dad was sitting in the wrought iron rocker outside under the carport and that he did not recognize her. I remembered that he had said that "some woman" had come to the house earlier; it never dawned on me that my husband would not remember that our daughter had come by the house that day. We did not know it at the time but Enoch had begun exhibiting behavior that was typical of the early stages of Alzheimer's.

The next 10 years of my life were filled with a mixture of sorrow and joy. I had not really experienced a death in my family that left me with a void since my baby Bernise had died. When my Mother died I knew that it was inevitable. She had a chronic heart condition and had worried herself to death over my brothers and sisters' wild adventures. When my Father died at the age of 75 in 1965, I cried at home because he had always taught us that Clarks were to be dignified at a funeral—it was a time of celebration. I remember his coming to the house to spend the weekend with me; he would always sit in his favorite chair with Peggie on his knee. He would tell her that when he was 75 and had suffered for all of his sins he would die. The last time we saw him he was all dressed up in a suit at a double funeral; two of Enoch's nephews had drowned. We talked to him after the funeral; he said he was going home to take a nap. I dismissed his statement and we loaded up the car to go home; we had just gotten back to Augusta when the phone rang. My sister told me that she found him dead lying on his bed. I would miss my Father but I would not cry out at his funeral. He had lived a full life on this earth and he was ready to meet his Maker. I was his oldest child; I knew that he would expect me to be strong for the others and I was determined that if he were looking down from heaven he would be proud of me.

Enoch got progressively worse; he did not know what he was doing half the time. He would go walking down the street and could not tell anybody where he was going or where he lived. Usually a neighbor would bring him back home. One morning one of the neighbors found him by the mailbox. I was fast asleep when I heard a young man's voice yelling, "Mrs. Ward, Mrs. Ward!" I jumped up out of bed and went out to find my husband being dragged into the house by a man and his son; Enoch's money was hanging out of his pockets and he was disoriented. I had them lay him on a daybed out in his little place. At this point I called my son and daughter, Enoch, Jr. and Peggie. At first they arranged for in-home healthcare assistants to come in to help with him; these women would not clean him because he refused to allow it. My other son, Wayne, came down and helped me give him a bath. But this was just the beginning. As time went by my husband's dementia progressed so much that I could not bear it. Enoch, Jr. agreed to place him in a Nursing Home.

It was September of 1995 when Enoch was placed in a Nursing Home. In the next few months my children would tell me that their Father did not know them; and yet I could walk into the room and he would recognize my voice and call out, "Renie, Renie, is that you?" I would go over to him reassuringly and say, "Yes". Many people do not realize how very completely Alzheimer's affects a person's entire physical and mental existence. Enoch lost control of his bodily functions first; next his body started to fail to know that it should fight disease so his immune system was weakened. A simple cut on his toe became infected and because he also had poor circulation he developed gangrene in his leg, which eventually spread all over his body. I had never seen this man, my husband of 64 years, have any pain and yet he was crying out to God for mercy. He had been Chairman of the Deacon Board at Rockyford Baptist Church, the church that his Mother and Father had helped build, for over 30 years. I had been by his side as the President of the Deaconess and later as the Mother of the Church. We had worked in the Church and tithed as good obedient Christians and God had blessed us both with very little illness. I had heard my husband pray many times, always beginning each prayer with the Lord's Prayer. But now he repeated the Lord's Prayer continuously. Enoch, Jr. had spoken to the doctors who had given little hope of any extended life span if his leg was amputated; he wanted the family to just keep his Dad comfortable and let him die. Peggie, on the other hand, was adamant that his leg should be removed to relieve him of the suffering. As his wife the final decision was mine. Grace had come home to visit her Dad; Peggie had explained the situation to Grace and the two of them arranged for me to see the leg. When I saw it I screamed out to the doctor, "Cut it off, cut it off!" Enoch came through the operation just fine. However, the doctor had been correct in that within a couple of months the other leg had to be amputated. Then there were sores on his back and the rest of his body that would not heal. The infection was quickly spreading and by December 30, 1995, my husband of 64 years died. There would be no traditional New Year's celebration this year; New Year's Eve was spent preparing for Enoch's funeral. It was cold and rainy and I cried at home. The month of January in 1996 had a dreadful beginning with ice and snowstorms all across the Eastern seaboard; by the grace of God all of the children made it safely home to their Father's funeral. The funeral was held with great fanfare—a salute and tribute to a Father who had worked and struggled to care for his wife and his children all of his life.

Little Charlie, the young man whose Father had employed my Enoch for so many years, handled my husband's funeral arrangements. Enoch lay in state at the Gilbert Lambuth Memorial Chapel at Paine College. The processional was beautiful; we walked in by two's, hand in hand, as we passed his coffin to honor him before we were seated. The audience stood as we marched down the aisle to pay tribute to this great husband, Father, and Christian. My son who had been called to the ministry, Enoch, Jr., preached his Father's funeral. He read the scripture about Enoch, comparing his Father to the servant in the Bible. He referenced Enoch's translation and referred to my Enoch's dementia—likening it to a walk with God from which he would periodically return. His death or translation was the final call from God for my Enoch to stay with God forever. I spoke about my husband and our life together; the Choir from Gloria's Church sang like angels from heaven. The program included a poem, "*I'm Free*", and the Choir sang the song by that name; my baby girl worked diligently with her brother and older sister to make the program a beautiful tribute to their Father. Now I had coached my children and told them that I expected them to cry at home and to show strong resolve at the funeral. Few were able to comply with my request. The funeral was attended by family and friends; and the Repast was held at the school down in East Augusta. My husband had not been educated beyond grade school so the children thought that a funeral at Paine College and Repast at the Middle School were appropriate. Enoch is buried at Hillcrest Memorial where I will be laid to rest beside him. I'm sure he was looking down from heaven smiling at the beautiful ceremony.

The next few years were tough. My oldest boy James had

been in an accident several years before; he had broken every bone in his back. I remember the incident as if it were just yesterday. I received a call from the hospital; the person told me that my son had been injured. I immediately took a quick bath and dressed myself real nice. My Dad had always stressed that you are who you are perceived to be—"*Always look nice and neat, you never know who you might meet*" was one of his favorite expressions. I walked into that emergency room and told them who I was—that I had received a call about my son. I found James laying there naked and moaning, begging for help. Because he was a construction worker who was dusty and unkempt the doctors and nurses were ignoring him. Well they obviously did not know that he was my son! I called and said, "Hey, somebody get in here and see about my son. That's my son in there! I want somebody to see about him!" In a matter of minutes they had him cleaned up and placed in a room with medication for pain. X-rays revealed that he had broken every bone in his backbone. The surgeons talked to us about the operation; the prognosis was not good. They would have to place pins up and down his spine; we were told that he would never walk again.

When I returned home I called the children. Bennie retained a lawyer to litigate James' case; he asked Peggie to work with the woman to handle all of the details. Bennie was determined that no matter the cost his older brother would have adequate compensation and medical care for the rest of his life. J.E. was awarded a settlement, which he received on a monthly basis after an initial lump sum; the contractor was responsible for all current and future medical bills related to the injury. In the meantime J.E. was determined to prove the surgeons wrong; he did walk and drive and do everything but not without severe pain. He would live with that pain for the rest of his life.

He and I were always very close; he was my firstborn and I turned all of my attention to him after Enoch died. I took care of his grocery shopping, his financial matters, everything.

Imagine that—an 83-year old woman taking care of her 63-year old son's affairs! It was a role that I had assumed since he had the accident. But now it was different; I depended on him and he depended on me. He gave me the motivation and desire to live; I was *needed!* The other children were here but James came to my house every day. If he missed a day he would call.

It was the week coming up to Labor Day in 1997 and all of us were getting ready for the Clark Family Reunion. Grace and Tammy had come home for the celebration. I had been sick earlier in the year and Peggie had taken me to the hospital. They did not keep me; they sent me home with some medicine. James had come down to my house on that Wednesday to get some of his money. The day before, he had gone from house to house banging on doors saying that his Mother was in the house—somebody had better break down the door because she was dead. Well I did not answer the door on Tuesday because I was not there; I had gone downtown to shop. He had come back on Wednesday to tell me what had happened. I was furious and told him never to have someone break into my house! He left grumbling but said that he would be back on Friday. I never saw him again. That Wednesday night he had a heart attack and died.

We all became preoccupied with getting ready for the reunion. We went down to Magnolia Springs; it was a beautiful Saturday and I enjoyed so much being around all of my family. We played games, ate plenty of food, and enjoyed seeing friends and family that we had not seen in years. When we returned Julia called Enoch, Jr. to tell him that James had been found dead. All of my children knew how much I loved him; they were afraid to tell me. The children discussed it and agreed that Peggie was the best person to tell me about J.E. It was late that night when she came into the door. Oh, how I look back on how awful it must have been for her to have to tell me. I screamed, "I'm not supposed to outlive my children; Lord, why?!" It seemed as if my whole world had come to an end—as if someone had taken a knife and literally cut out a piece of my heart. And what made it so difficult for me was that I never got to see him. It was so hot in his house when he died; he did not have a single window or door open when he laid down that night. It was ironic that his door had to be pried open when just a few days before he had suggested prying my door open to my neighbors. Rev. Ward would later say that the Lord had given us a sign—a warning—but we did not understand it. It was tragic; his body had deteriorated so badly from the heat that viewing was not allowed. Imagine the heartbreak! My firstborn was dead and I could not even see him one last time before they put him in the ground! Oh how I wept!

James had a beautiful graveside service at Hillcrest Memorial Park. He was buried in a plot right next to his Dad. James' funeral was also preached by his brother, Rev. Enoch Ward, Jr. Several of the children were here for the funeral; his ex-wife Thelma and his daughter Edwina were there along-with other family members and friends. Grace, Kathy, and Irene were already here with their families for the reunion; Joann and Bennie and his wife Gabi came home to pay their last respects. Peggie and Enoch, Jr. took care of the arrangements for his funeral and the Repast, which was held at our Church. The two men that meant the most to me had been taken from me; I was lost. Sometimes I would lay across my bed and the other side of the bed would appear to sink down as if someone were sitting beside me; I could feel and smell Enoch's presence in my room. It was as if he came back to comfort me. I would eventually fall off to sleep; after a while I stopped having the visits. My faith in God and the hereafter brought me to a place where I understand that I will see them both again. Don't get me wrong! My heart still aches for them both at times but the beautiful memories that I hold of the times we shared together quickly replace my tears of sorrow with tears of joy. I am so grateful for our lives together. Oh how we did live!

At the time I did not understand it but I later came to realize that God took J.E. because he knew my future; without me to take care of him James would not have survived. And I was about to begin a battle with my own physical health that would require every bit of my strength and resolve to endure. Through it all I have reminded myself over and over again that God does not make mistakes. Where would I be without God?

The More Things Change

There is an old saying that the more things change the more they remain the same. It's true you know. I can remember when we were children and even after we moved to Augusta that there were no bolts or locks on doors. People knocked before they entered your house; they waited for you to say, "Come on in", before they walked through your door. If you visited someone they offered you a bite to eat and you ate it. The children were not afraid to play outside and children were not allowed to stay out late at night; men worked while women stayed at home to take care of the children. If children misbehaved they were spanked and if they cried loud it was okay; nobody called the police or yelled child abuse.

The man was man of the house; the woman he married was his wife and mother to their children. If they were happy they stayed together; if they were unhappy they stayed together. Divorce was something you read about or saw on television. The man worked and provided for his home; whatever he brought in was what you had and you were glad for it. Children respected their parents and obeyed them; parents respected their children and supported them. And if a neighbor saw your child doing something wrong s/he spanked him; you did not go over to beat or curse the neighbor because s/he hit your child. Teachers were encouraged to discipline your child when he was wrong; if you were called to the school because of something your child did he got another spanking because he should know better than to cause trouble in school. And the school was not sued. Imagine that!

It was a simpler time when people had values, morals, and pride. God was recognized as a sovereign being who was merciful and mighty. Children were taught to love and respect God, themselves, and others. And with that came respect for their property and the property of others. Children were loved, cherished, and nurtured but also disciplined. Men were satisfied with being men; and women had no problems being women. We had pride in who we were and where we came from and we knew where we were going. We dared to dream and had the faith, stamina, and perseverance to see our dreams realized. We taught our children through the lives that we lived, by our example. Our children prayed because they saw us pray. They were eager to work because they saw us work. They were responsible, because they saw us be responsible. They shared because they saw us share. They cared because they saw us care. They loved each other and us because they saw us love each other and them. And we opened our windows breathed fresh air at night and enjoyed just being alive. Everyday was new—full of challenges and opportunities, which we gladly greeted. We pressed on toward the prize on higher ground!

When my last two children, Grace and Peggie, left home I was 58 years old and Enoch was 64; by the time Peggie became a sophomore in college her Dad was 65 years old and eligible for Social Security. He could have retired but he worked as a grocery store manager for Charlie Reid; he was so used to working all of his life it would have probably resulted in an early death if he had stopped working. And as for me I worked in the house and in my flower and vegetable gardens; I sewed quilts for all of my children and cooked meals (like I was still cooking for a house full) until I figured out how to cut my recipes in half! By the time I reached the age of 65 I had been to the Social Security Administration and Department of Social Services offices for the various Medical cards offered. My husband and I had few illnesses that required serious medical attention so our use of medical services was restricted to a yearly physical checkup and assistance with a few prescription medicines. We always took pride in the fact that although we had ten children when we arrived in Augusta we seldom went hungry and we never accepted handouts or food stamps. The thought never crossed our minds because we were brought up believing in ourselves—that what we could not provide God would provide. And because we had that attitude we always had plenty to share with others and we gave it freely. As I look back on our lives together, even though we had our fair share of trials and tribulations, we never blamed anyone else for our circumstances or plight. We always took responsibility for our own welfare. And we accomplished great things—through faith in God, hard work, perseverance, and faith in ourselves.

It saddens my heart to see what has happened to black families today. We say that we were freed from slavery before 1900 and yet one hundred years later in the year 2000 we are products of a new kind of enslavement, one that we have created for ourselves. Young black women sit at home and have babies to collect welfare while black men lay around eating and sleeping, contributing nothing but negative values to the household. Black women who do work often end up taking care of the family. And even in homes where both the man and the woman work the children are left to bring up themselves. Poor children, they have no positive role models. Parents do not teach them about the love of God and Christ Jesus. If they learned to love God, to understand that He loves them, and that Christ is in them they would learn to love themselves. The children do not realize that He is their source and their guide. They grow up hungry and cold—not from lack of food or heat but from the lack of the nourishment and warmth that comes from a loving father and mother. We cannot blame our plight on racism. You see too many parents fail to realize that if their children are introduced to God they can always have a Father; they can always have love, food, and shelter—God will supply all their needs. Even when parents cannot be there for the children He is there. He will protect them for you; and He'll erase their fears and dry their tears.

Every parent has his or her own ideas about the best way to bring up a child. After 10 children and over 40 years of child rearing I have observed that each child is different; therefore, a good parent must individualize the parenting process for each child. And yet regardless of individual differences the basic needs that children have are the same irrespective of personality, background, or station in life. How a parent responds to those needs can really impact the child's self esteem and his or her outlook on life. Over the years I have identified at least *12 Secrets for Successful Parenting*. Let me share them with you.

1. ***Put God First.*** Introduce your children to God and His son, Jesus Christ. Tell them about God through Biblical stories, scripture, prayer, and song. Make sure that they understand His love for all of us, and tell them that they, like you, are made in His image. Introduce them to the Church and encourage their participation in Church activities; this is the best way of teaching them about praising and serving God and helping their fellow man. This step helps the child to have a good foundation for living.
2. ***Teach Your Children Their Heritage.*** Teach your children about their family. Help them to learn as much as

possible about their grandparents, aunts, uncles, sisters, brothers, and cousins—the whole family tree. Even if you are a single parent tell them about their biological *other parent* and his or her lineage. It is very important that children have a sense of belonging and it is an important step in their development to have a sense of self. It's okay if the parent isn't physically there; share with them the good things that you know about the person. And if you complete #1 above successfully they will already know that they have a rich heritage and inheritance through Christ Jesus and that they are a member of His family (Christians); so the impact of a missing parent can be put in its proper perspective. This step helps the child to be well founded in life.

3. ***Teach Your Children Their Roles.*** By this I mean that children need to understand that YOU are the parent and that THEY are the children. From the time that babies first learn to move they start to challenge you. They will love you more if you set boundaries for them and explain that they must follow your rules. This is key to having obedient children; and if they are disobedient dare to discipline them (as Dr. Dobson would say)! They will thank you for it one day because if you do not teach them about authority, rules, and obedience at home the world will teach them.

4. ***Teach Your Children Responsibility.*** In every story that I have ever told about my children you can see how the children were delegated certain responsibilities. From the time that they were young each one was encouraged and wanted to share in the upkeep and maintenance of our home. Enoch and I took pride in what we had accumulated and what we had accomplished; our children naturally had that same pride. I never asked my girls to wash dishes or to cook; they saw me doing it and asked me to show them how. The boys wanted to help with the farm, the yard, and other chores. When

they had been taught how to do these things we delegated responsibilities to each of them and made the older ones overseers of the younger children's efforts. We showed them that our family was a team whose success was dependent on each person completing the tasks that they were assigned; and we taught them to be responsible for each other—so that if a sibling needed help to complete his or her tasks the help was freely given. Teaching a child to be responsible at home will make all the difference in his ability to be responsible in life.

5. **Start When They Are Young.** The most important thing for parents to do is to begin training the child early— the earlier the better! Start reading and singing to your children (# 1) as soon as they are born. Read stories that are based on biblical and good life principles; sing songs of praise and worship. Pray for your children and allow them to see and hear you pray even before they can utter a word; you can even do this while they are in your womb! As soon as they can talk begin teaching them to pray and to sing songs of praise. The Bible is a wonderful source of stories that teach lessons for successful living. As soon as they can read help them with these stories; read along with them and take the time to help them understand what they have read. By doing this your children will learn to obey God and to obey you! If they are taught when they are young when they are older they won't forget it!

6. **Teach Your Children that Failure is a Part of Life.** Keep in mind that while you want your children to be successful, you also want them to understand that a failure is not the end of the world. In fact they should be taught to learn from their mistakes and how to turn an obstacle into an opportunity. Don't compare them to others inside or outside of the family; don't belittle them. Instead encourage them; be there for

them to help and guide them through each failure as a learning process. As my Dad used to say, "*the most important part of the falling down is the getting up*".

7. ***Keep the Lines of Communication Open.*** Most parents are always trying to talk to their children to provide unsolicited advice. I don't know about you but I can't hear you when I am talking; I'm too busy concentrating on what I'm about to say. Children need good listeners. If you will listen to them they will come to you when they need your advice and yes they will ASK for it. They may even come to you when they really don't need advice; they will come to you just because they respect your opinion. Just think about this. You and I go to God, our heavenly Father, whenever we need to because we know that He hears us; we freely ask Him for anything because we trust and have faith in HIM. We feel that way because even though He allows us to make our own choices (and oftentimes they are not the greatest), when everything goes bad in our lives we know He is still there and that He loves us—unconditionally. We know that His communication lines are open and so we go to Him all the time. If we use God's behavior towards us as our example we can have a similar relationship with our children.

8. ***Help Them to Define and Achieve Their Goals, Not Yours.*** This one is tough because oftentimes parents see so much of themselves in their children; they just naturally want them to achieve the things they were never able to accomplish. Back Off! Encourage them to experiment and experience all that is good that life has to offer—to expand their horizons to include places and things to which you may never have been exposed. You have given them the tools (# 1-7) to be able to recover from their mistakes. Let them find their place in the scheme of things; allow them to make decisions and teach them to accept the

responsibility and the consequences for the decisions that they make. Be there for them if they need you—and they will. Life is a learning experience; allow them to live it abundantly!

9. ***Love your Children Unconditionally.*** Nothing is more disheartening for a child than to feel as if s/he is loved on condition. Accept the fact that your children have their own personalities, strengths, and weaknesses; if you have more than one child realize that no two children are alike. Do NOT compare them! God has given each one of them at least one talent; some children have more than others. Help your children to identify their gift; then do all you can to help them to cultivate and use it. If they never do anything love them anyway. Love them just because . . . for no reason except that they are gifts from God! Tell them you love them every day and night—as often as you can; write them love letters. When my children were away in school I wrote them short letters of encouragement that always ended with "Love, Mom". I remembered their birthdays and other special occasions; if they gave me a gift I wrote them a personal note of thanks. I called them—not too often—but enough to show them that I care. With today's technology parents and siblings can keep in touch with each other with e-mail. My daughter stays in touch with her brothers and sisters using the computer. It doesn't matter how you do it just do it! As your children begin to *believe* that both God and you love them unconditionally they will become more secure and self-confident.

10. ***Teach Your Children to Love and Respect You and Themselves.*** Once your children know who they are and their heritage and you have shown them in word and in deed that you just love them, just as they are, they will in turn reciprocate. The key here is to recognize and reinforce their displays of affection. This

takes time and effort because no two people will display affection in the same way. Yes, it means you have to take time to look beyond the outer child to his inner soul. How can you do this? Spend time with him or her. Learn to enjoy some of the things that s/he enjoys. Become an active participant in his or her life; don't just sit and watch the years go by! Be your child's advocate and cheer leader. Promote him when he does something good; lovingly chastise and discipline him when he does something bad. Teach him about his worth to God and to you; from your example he will learn his own self-worth. Respect is handled in much the same way; if you want to get it you have to give it. Respect yourselves and show respect to your children and they in turn will reciprocate.

11. *Teach Your Children to Choose Their Company.* The first thing that parents have to do is build a good foundation of values and morals for their children as a basis—one that they can use as a measuring stick for others. If you are successful in steps (#1-10), your children will have no problem determining (for themselves) whether the people they spend time with are *good* company. They must develop their own set of criteria and yes—you must allow them to go through the process. The earlier you start the better. If you always choose the people your children hang around, when they are older they are bound to choose people you would NOT choose as their pals. Allow them to make choices while they are at home under your roof. Invite their friends into your home so that you know the choices that they make. Offer advice only if asked or if it becomes necessary. And no, they will not always make the right choices; but if you are there when they discover their mistakes and you have left the lines of communication open you'll be able to help them to learn from their experiences and to healthily move on.

12. *Lead By Example.* The best way to show someone how to do anything is for you to do it, allowing the person to watch you every step of the way. Your children watch you whether you like it or not. When you do something right they see it; and if you do something wrong they see that, too! So try to *live* the best example that you can live before them! Do that by walking in faith. And when you make a mistake don't hide it. Let them see you admit that you made a mistake; show them through your example how to get up and move on when you fall. If its hard let them see the difficulty—but show them how perseverance and persistence pays off in the end! Your children need to know that you are not perfect and that you don't expect them to be perfect! They need to see you pray and worship God. They need to see you live without fear walking in faith and obedience to God. And they *will* follow your lead!

Now as you proceed through these steps you must stay in prayer. Some steps may be more difficult to achieve than others; and some children are slower to catch on than others. And some children may never get it right! It's okay. You do your part—train them up and be there for them—then take them to God; present them before Him as His children. Claim Him and His salvation for them and He will guide and direct all of your paths. Oh, if only the black folk of this day and time knew my Savior! What a revelation and restoration our race would see!

Twilight and Evening Star

Enoch loved to make sure that our yards were well groomed and immaculate; he wanted the house to be clean and there to be plenty of food for any one who happened to stop by. After his death, my children visited me regularly but my neighbors were the real source of strength and encouragement. My remaining sisters and brother (Buddy) came to see me often; there was always food on the stove and in the refrigerator. Over the next few years I did my best to maintain our home in a manner that was befitting for the neighborhood and that would be pleasing to Enoch. I was reconciled with the loss of my husband and my firstborn. But *"death always comes in three's"*, the old people would say. And so it was; my son Lee Mark died a mysterious death in his condominium in Los Angeles. His estranged wife sent his body home for a graveside service in Augusta that she did not attend. His body was carried to the gravesite via Rolls Royce; his brother, Rev. Ward, preached the sermon. The Repast was held at the Sheraton Hotel. Billy, as Lee Mark had been called, loved the finer things in life. He owned a Rolls Royce, a Jaguar, a home in Woodland Hills, and now a home and condominium in upper LA. His wife had seen to it that he was *put away* nicely. His Uncle Buddy, his Aunt Julia, his sisters Joann, Peggie, Irene, and Grace, were all here for the funeral. Several of Lee Mark's classmates stopped by to pay respects to him at the funeral home. It was obvious that many had loved him; I'm sure Billy was pleased at the ceremony. After the ceremony his body was flown back to LA where he was interred in Forest Lawn near his son high above the gravesites below overlooking the entire city. I am told that my daughter-in-law has roses sent to his gravesite every month as a tribute to him for the many years of love and laughter they shared.

"Enough!" my daughter Joann said. She came home to get me, brought me a package of airline tickets for several round-trips to my choice of location, and accompanied me to Detroit to see my younger sister Emma. It was the trip of a lifetime; I enjoyed seeing her so much. Emma and I always had a ball; we were both older and in declining health but it was still like old times. From Detroit Joann and I flew out to California where I stayed another week with her and Charles. Next I flew home then over to see Grace, Irene, and Katherine (in Maryland, New York, and New Jersey) and finally out to see Joann again.

In the meantime my son-in-law Tom, who is Joann's husband, repaired everything he found broken in my house; he painted, cleaned, did whatever was necessary to restore the little brick cottage to its normal state. My next visit to California was on Mother's Day; Joann had a sit down meal that was catered with hundreds of guests to honor me on Mother's Day. She sent out beautiful invitations and there was a program with presentations. Several of the children came including Grace, Katherine, and Tammy. We all drove up to San Francisco where I ate in China Town, crossed over the Golden Gate Bridge, and saw numerous other tourist attractions. During this time I also flew over to see Bennie in Knoxville. I was seldom at home; my children kept me traveling from one of their homes to the next. And I enjoyed every bit of it. I always loved to travel; I seemed to be able to lose myself in the beautiful surroundings. And the air seemed to make me feel better when I was away from home.

The next few years I spent at my home with an occasional trip to visit my relatives or children. I would clean, cook, and spend time tending to my garden. I contracted a man to keep my yards clean and neat just as I did when Enoch was alive. And I got up on ladders and climbed up to clean straw off my roof. I went shopping and took care of all of my financial and personal affairs. I love flowers; my yard was full of roses, lilies, lilacs, begonias, tulips, and cacti. I had a beautiful Christmas cactus that I had grown in my Florida Room. But the most beautiful set of flowering cacti were strategically located at each end of the front of my yard; they produced gorgeous yellow blooms in springtime.

When my neighbor gave me the cacti they were small; within a very short period of time they had grown so large that they were no longer manageable. They were taller and wider than I had ever imagined and because of their prickly sprouts I could not water any of the flowers that were planted nearby. The spring of 1998 I decided to prune these flowers. As a result I had little prickles in every part of my body from head to toe, even though my body was completely covered during the pruning process. As was usual I took (I had to drag them because of their weight) the cut pieces of the plants to an open space in the back yard and burned them; I sat alongside the fire watching ever so closely so that it did not get out of control. Later in the week I started to begin to feel the prickles; Peggie saw me picking the needles from my skin. "Mom, what are you doing?", she asked. I told her what happened; she was so upset—not just about the prickles but about the whole idea that I had cut the cacti, dragged them into the back yard, and burned them. Oh, how she fussed. But you know the older I got the more I needed so very much to hold onto some semblance of independence. My children were off living their lives; my grandchildren were young men and women enjoying their lives. Since Enoch and James were no longer with me my life's focus was serving God and keeping my house, flowers, and yard nice. Anyway, I finally got to the point that my muscles began to atrophy—that is they started to just disappear. Peggie immediately blamed it on the cacti.

At first I would stand and it was as if my legs would suddenly just collapse—they were no longer there to support me. I would end up scooting down on the floor to break the fall. The children got a walking stick for me; I needed a walker but my pride would not allow me to use it in public. Next of course I used the walker; in the interim I had every test imaginable performed. My children offered to move me into an assisted living facility; I refused. My home was the last remaining piece of my life with my family; I had planned to stay there until I died. Well God had other plans; since I refused to listen to any of the servants (my children) whom He sent to help me transition from my old home to the new place he had for me He decided to give me a wake up call—a little reminder that He was still in control.

Now during this time I became a tremendous responsibility for Enoch, Jr., and Peggie. They took turns coming over to feed me and make sure that I was okay during the week; a healthcare assistant came every weekday to care for me, cook, wash laundry, and clean up the house. At night I stayed alone; I had a security system with a panic button around my neck and one on the wall beside my bed. I had a programmed portable phone and a portable toilet so that I did not have to leave my room to use the bathroom at night. The children had gotten me a Mini Jazzy electric wheel chair with a joystick control, which I learned to maneuver throughout my home. And they had a ramp built to provide access in and out of my house so that I could go outside to look at my flowers whenever I wanted. My home was wheelchair accessible inside and out! On Saturday's Peggie came to make sure I had warm food to eat and to see to other personal details; Enoch, Jr. came on Sunday's after Church. The other children came home when they could to help. I had it made, right? Wrong! One evening just after Peggie and Wayne had left me to retire for the night, I scooted the short distance from my bed to the portable toilet and fell. Now they did not know it but I had fallen several times before; each time I had been able to pull myself up. Except for a little soreness I was fine by the next morning. This time I could not move; I knew that if I did not call 911, I would just have to stay there until the children came the next day. I thought I was having a stroke or heart attack!

The only thing I could recall was my brother Buddy telling me about his first heart attack. He said that something hit him and he was lying sprawling on the floor. He could see and hear everything that was happening, but he could not articulate to his wife what he was thinking and he could not move. She looked at him and started screaming and crying; but instead of calling 911, she called everyone of his kids, his sisters, brothers, her family—everybody but 911! He said he wanted to scream, "Call 911, woman! Call 911!". He jokingly said that he thought he would surely die before she ever called for help; finally she called. I laughed about this story when it was being told but then realized how very helpless he must have felt. I had that same feeling for a moment but then with determination decided that if I could just shift my body I could grab the phone and punch 911 with my cane. And so I did; luckily the EMT's were met by caring neighbors, one of whom I had given a key to my house. Lisa let them in and called Peggie, who met me at the hospital. She called Enoch, Jr. and as usual he came immediately. In this crisis my loving family comforted me.

Old people and black folks catch it in hospitals! I am so thankful to God that he did not take my speech or my mind during that incident; I would be dead by now. I kept telling the idiots at that hospital that I needed some tests or something; they kept saying that there was nothing wrong. Peggie came and called my doctor at the time who said that the EMT's had taken me to the *wrong* hospital (there should be no such thing), so therefore he could not practice or provide any input on the attending physician's diagnosis. I refused to go home; the hospital refused to keep me. I told my children to take me to a Nursing Home; I asked them not to leave me alone at night in my house until they found one.

Enoch, Jr. stayed with me for two nights while he searched for a suitable Nursing Home. Now the Nursing Home that accepted me is one of the best in the area. It was by the grace of God that I was placed there since they have a waiting list a mile long most of the time. Peggie would not agree to my being placed in the home unless it met with her approval; Enoch, Jr. had her visit the place. After reviewing the physical structure, facilities, and talking with personnel, she completed a review of the Nursing Home's ratings (on the Internet). She agreed that the place was suitable. She drove me over to the Nursing Home; afterwards she came over every morning and evening until she learned all the names and faces of the people who would interact with me on a daily basis. Peggie, Enoch, Jr., and Wayne stayed right by my side through this ordeal; and God led me right to the place where he intended for me to stay. As we approached the entrance Peggie said, "Mom, did you see all the beautiful begonias?" Of course I could not sit up to see them that day. "Oh, Mom, it looks as if God handpicked this place just for you!" She was right; He did!

When I got to the Nursing Home I could not move my legs or hands. I had to wait for someone—a Nurse or Nurse's Assistant (CAN)—to turn me over, to feed me, to do everything. They determined almost immediately that I had not had a stroke. They allowed me to have time to get

PEGGIE WARD KOON, PH.D.

acclimated to my surroundings. My baby daughter saw my
frustration and asked them to start therapy. The first therapist
that worked with me was very young; she told Peggie that I
had all the symptoms of a spinal cord injury. I had already
been told that my spine was twisted at the base, a condition
that doctors believed I had from birth. This young lady
thought that when I fell I jarred my already twisted spine
just enough to severely injure it; all my motor functions below
my neck were affected. When I moved my hands it was in a
jerky kind of way. But this therapist, with the support and
persistence of my children, nurtured me and aggressively
worked with me until I could begin to control my movement
in my hands. From that point forward I have been steadily
making progress. I can feed myself, turn over, call my
daughter on the phone, and even write letters. I am so
blessed to have made this much progress in so short a time.
I attribute my progress to Faith in God, Faith in myself, and
the Clark desire to be independent and strong—to turn
adversity into opportunity.

The Bible says that you are only promised 3 score and 10
years on this earth which men interpret to mean 70 years.
My parents always told me that your conduct, that is your
behavior, could shorten or lengthen your days. If that is true
then God must be pleased with all that I have done for I
have exceeded the allotted time in this place. God blessed
me to grow up in a wonderful loving family, with a Father
who was a positive inspiring role model. I married Enoch
Ward, a devoted, loving, God-fearing man who was a good
husband and Father who provided for my children and me.
I am so proud that God blessed our union so that we had 11
wonderful healthy children; He allowed us to live to see all
of them except one live to achieve their goals. God blessed
our children so that they have been prosperous, allowing
them to reach goals that have more than exceeded any of
our expectations. God also blessed us with the joy of lovingly
influencing the character and make-up of our beautiful

140

grandchildren; we were allowed to watch them mature and grow into responsible young men and women. And we lived in a community of loving and caring neighbors who were there for us when we needed them most.

My name is Irene Clark Ward. I am the firstborn of James Clark, the second daughter of James Clark and Ina Mae Chandler, and the wife of the late Enoch Ward, Sr. I have been blessed beyond measure these past 88 years. I have eight loving and wonderfully successful children that are still living. These are my sons: James E. Ward, Deceased; Charles M. Ward, a former Electrical Engineer for Rockwell International & Northrop Aero Space; Lee Mark Ward, Deceased; Rev. Enoch Ward, Jr., Pastor of the First Metropolitan Baptist Church and former Vice President of Proctor and Gamble; and Dr. Bennie F.L. Ward, Nuclear Physicist and Professor who has lectured and completed research in countries around the world, including Jerusalem. These are my daughters: Grace Ward Gray, former head teacher, business woman, and franchise owner; Bernise Ward, Deceased; Irene Sua, Director of Hospital Administration; Katherine Ward Brown, Elementary school teacher; Joann Ward Ogburn, Engineering Manager for Boeing and former Engineering Manager for Rockwell International; and Dr. Peggie Ward Koon, IS Manager, Adjunct Professor, and Author.

In addition to being loved by my family I have received the love of my fellow man; everywhere I have ever gone I have greeted and been greeted by others with a smile. Now that's living!